ANTHROPOLOGY, POLITICS, AND THE STATE

In recent years anthropology has rediscovered its interest in politics. Building on the findings of this research, this book offers a new way of analysing the relationship between culture and politics, with special attention to democracy, nationalism, the state, and political violence. Beginning with scenes from an unruly early 1980s election campaign in Sri Lanka, it covers issues from rural policing in North India to slum housing in Delhi, presenting arguments about secularism and pluralism, and the ambiguous energies released by electoral democracy across the subcontinent. It ends by discussing feminist peace activists in Sri Lanka, struggling to sustain a window of shared humanity after two decades of war. Bringing together and linking the themes of democracy, identity and conflict, this important new study shows how anthropology can take a central role in understanding other people's politics, especially the issues that seem to have divided the world since 9/11.

JONATHAN SPENCER is Professor of the Anthropology of South Asia at the University of Edinburgh. His previous books include *A Sinhala Village in a Time of Trouble: Politics and Change in Rural Sri Lanka* (1990); *Sri Lanka: History and the Roots of Conflict* (1990), *Encyclopedia of Social and Cultural Anthropology* (co-edited with Alan Barnard, 1996), and *The Conditions of Listening: Essays on Religion, History and Politics in South Asia* (co-edited with C. J. Fuller, 1996),

Anthropology, Politics, and the State

Democracy and Violence in South Asia

JONATHAN SPENCER
University of Edinburgh

CAMBRIDGE UNIVERSITY PRESS
Cambridge, New York, Melbourne, Madrid, Cape Town, Singapore, São Paulo

Cambridge University Press
The Edinburgh Building, Cambridge CB2 8RU, UK

Published in the United States of America by Cambridge University Press, New York

www.cambridge.org
Information on this title: www.cambridge.org/9780521777469

© Jonathan Spencer 2007

First published 2007

Printed in the United Kingdom at the University Press, Cambridge

A catalogue record for this publication is available from the British Library

ISBN 978-0-521-77177-1 hardback
ISBN 978-0-521-77746-9 paperback

For Janet and Jessica for everything

Contents

List of illustrations

Acknowledgements

This book is the product of many conversations over the years. Parts of it have been presented in seminars and workshops in Cambridge, Colombo, Edinburgh, Gothenberg, Harvard, Heidelberg, London, New Orleans, Oxford, Paris, and Peradeniya. I am grateful to the late Raj Chandavarkar, the late Neelan Tiruchelvam, Radhika Coomaraswamy, Goran Aijmer, Arthur Kleinman, the late Richard Burghart, Robert Gibb, Mattison and Gill Mines and Mayfair Yang, Tudor Silva, Sudipta Kaviraj, and David Washbrook for their hospitality on these occasions. The annual meetings of the South Asian Anthropologists' Group have not only provided an audience for parts of this work in progress on more occasions than I care to remember; they have also kept me in touch with some of the most exciting and fresh research from emerging scholars, research which has in some cases found its way into the chapters that follow. I am especially grateful to three of its most active members, Mukulika Banerjee, Lucia Michelutti, and Arild Ruud for kindly allowing me to use photographs from their own path-breaking research on South Asian politics. The arguments in this book grew (in rather unpredictable and unruly ways) out of the Malinowski Memorial Lecture which I gave at the London School of Economics in 1995: my thanks to the Department of Anthropology, and especially Chris Fuller and Jonathan Parry, for the invitation to deliver that lecture, and much else besides over the years. My friends in the Centre for South Asian Studies at Edinburgh, especially

Acknowledgements

Paul Dundas, Tony Good, Hugo Gorringe, Roger and Patricia Jeffery, and Crispin Bates, have provided a constant source of interdisciplinary stimulation, while my colleagues in Social Anthropology have been supportive and stimulating in appropriate proportion. I have been especially lucky to have worked alongside a small group of people in Edinburgh who have been doing genuinely path-breaking anthropological work on broadly political topics, notably Thomas Hansen, Iris Jean-Klein, Heonik Kwon and Yael Navaro-Yashin, Tony Good, and recently Kimberley Coles and Toby Kelly. I must also thank all the wonderful graduate students I have worked with in Edinburgh, especially in recent years Premakumara de Silva, Sharika Thiranagama, and Becky Walker.

In conversations over the years, a number of academic friends have – sometimes, I suspect, unwittingly – convinced me that the idea of a book on this theme was not entirely barmy: notably, at different times, Mukulika Banerjee, Richard Burghart, Veena Das, Thomas Hansen, Sudipta Kaviraj, Sunil Khilnani, and David Washbrook. Thomas found time in his breath-takingly full life to read a complete draft and provide helpful suggestions at an especially psychologically vulnerable moment.

The immediate stimulus for this work was the award of a Research Fellowship from the Nuffield Foundation. I am grateful to them for their wonderfully un-bureaucratic and patient support. My original fieldwork in Sri Lanka was carried out with the support of the then Social Science Research Council (now the ESRC), and return visits since 1991 have been supported by University of Edinburgh research and travel funds, and the British Council.

Parts of chapter two first appeared in *Journal des Anthropologues* 92–3: 31–49 (2003), and parts of chapter four were published in *Political Ritual,* edited by A. Boholm (Gothenburg, IASA, 1996), and a longer version was translated into Spanish as 'La democracia como sistema cultural' (Democracy as a Cultural System) and published in *Antropologica* 7: 5–28. An early version of chapter seven was presented to an international meeting in Colombo to celebrate the life of the Tamil politician and human rights activist Neelan Tiruchelvam who was assassinated by a suicide bomber in 1999. A copy of that presentation was subsequently published without permission in a daily newspaper in Sri Lanka, provoking a lengthy rebuttal from a leading nationalist ideologue, published under the heart-warming headline: Spencer Sponsors Tamil Racism. 'Cheerful laughter is our response', as Brecht's Galileo put it on another, not entirely dissimilar, occasion.

Charles Hallisey and Jayadeva Uyangoda have been with me through thick and thin, and it is fair to say that both this book, and its author, would not be in the shape they are in today without their remarkable capacity for friendship. Janet Carsten and Jessica Spencer have been there throughout the writing, and have endured the consequent moments of abstraction as best they could. When I realized parts of the argument were as old as Jessica herself I was reminded of a story about my old teacher Barney Cohn. When a veteran Chicago graduate student bumped into Barney one day and excitedly told him that he thought he was almost 'finished' on his dissertation, Barney replied 'Sometimes you shouldn't try to "finish". Sometimes you just have to stop.'

ONE

〇ᘿ

The Strange Death of Political Anthropology

What happened to the anthropology of politics? A subdiscipline which had seemed moribund in the 1980s has moved back to the centre of anthropological argument. Political themes – nationalism, conflict, citizenship – inflect exciting new work across (and beyond) the disciplinary spectrum. Where have these themes come from and what issues do they raise for anthropology in general? This book seeks to take stock of the recent political turn in anthropology, identifying key themes and common problems, while setting an agenda for work to come. In the pages that follow, I do not argue for any particular theoretical orthodoxy, but instead try to stage a dialogue between critical social and political theory and – anthropology's great strength – equally critical empirical research. The empirical research I concentrate on comes predominantly from one part of the world, South Asia, especially India and Sri Lanka, where particularly fruitful conversations have taken place between activists and intellectuals, and amongst representatives of different academic disciplines – especially history, political theory, and anthropology.

These conversations have taken place in years of upheaval. The critical events in India include the rise of Sikh separatism in the Punjab in the early 1980s, culminating in the assault on the Golden Temple in Amritsar in 1984, followed soon after by the assassination of Indira Gandhi and the wave of anti-Sikh violence which followed it; the destruction of the Babri

1

Masjid mosque in Ayodhya in 1992, and the Hindu–Muslim clashes which followed that; and the rise to national power of the right-wing Hindu Bharatiya Janata Party (BJP). In Sri Lanka, violence against the minority Tamil population in 1984 precipitated a decline into civil war between the government and the separatist Liberation Tigers of Tamil Ealam (LTTE). Indian intervention in 1987 sparked further schisms, this time between the government and a radical Sinhala youth party, the Janata Vimukti Peramuna (JVP): in the late 1980s thousands were killed or disappeared in this dispute. The war with the LTTE rumbled through the 1990s until both sides agreed a ceasefire in 2002, since when low-level violence has continued in parts of the country. Nepal, which supplies a third strand of material for my argument, has in the same period seen a self-consciously democratic revolution, and the rise of violent Maoist insurgency, as well as the bizarre slaughter of the king and other members of royal family in 2002. Unruly times, indeed.

We live in a world in which it has become brutally apparent that our collective survival depends on the ability to understand, and sometimes to anticipate, the strange world of other people's politics. (And, yes, the first problem is pinning down who 'we' might be, and asking just who 'other people' are, in formulations like this.) To achieve this, we need to pay sympathetic attention to the workings of apparently different versions of the political in places with different histories, and apparently different visions of justice and order. Anthropology is an academic discipline apparently well suited to this task, and in recent years it has made notable contributions to the interpretation of, among many other topics, religious violence in India, civil war in Sierra Leone, post-Apartheid processes of reconciliation in South Africa, the 'magical' aura of the secularist state in Turkey, and Islamic visions of democracy in Indonesia.[1]

---

[1] For example Richards on war in Sierra Leone, Wilson on truth and reconciliation in South Africa, Das and Hansen on religious violence in India, Navaro-Yashin on Turkey, Hefner on Islamism in Indonesia (Das 1990a; Das 1995b; Richards 1996; Hansen 1999; Hefner 2000; Hansen 2001b; Wilson 2001; Navaro-Yashin 2002).

The themes of this work – democracy, secularism, citizenship, nationalism and the nation-state, war and peace – are the big themes of political modernity. They are, though, somewhat different from the central themes of the subdiscipline known as political anthropology in the 1950s and 1960s, as a glance through the index of Joan Vincent's authoritative *Anthropology and Politics* (Vincent 1990) will confirm. Something has changed. In 1996 Vincent herself introduced a short overview of the field with the valedictory observation that political anthropology had been a 'late and comparatively short-lived subfield specialization within social and cultural anthropology' (Vincent 1996b: 428). The political turn in anthropology since the 1980s, which is the subject of this book, has been fuelled by external intellectual influences, from poststructural theorists of power, most obviously Michel Foucault, to postcolonial critics of the politics of representation, most notably Edward Said. It has, though, equally been shaped by global political developments, like the resurgence of religious and ethnic conflict in different parts of the world in the post-Cold War era. A casual reader of Vincent's later anthology on *The Anthropology of Politics* (Vincent 2002) would be hard pressed to identify what intellectual unity bound the short extract from Edmund Leach's micro-analysis of land conflict in 1950s Sri Lanka, with Gayatri Spivak's closing piece, which offers a poststructural commentary on Marx, the Enlightenment, and the politics of girls' schooling in rural Bangladesh (Leach 2002 [1961]; Spivak 2002 [1992]). Each of these perfectly sums up the intellectual-political sensibility of its time: the first is scrupulously empirical and morally detached from the people whose machinations it analyses, the other is equally scrupulously theoretical and overtly morally engaged with its subjects. Something indeed has changed.

Let me, though, start my story where it started for me: in Sri Lanka in 1982.

Before the underpants, obviously enough, came the sarong. In the early 1980s Cyril de Silva was a minor government official in an out of

3

the way village in Sri Lanka. He owed his position to his links to the ruling political party, the United National Party (UNP), which had come to power in 1977. As a man of local substance, his normal style of dress was the postcolonial bureaucratic trouser. But when his party's candidate won the 1982 Presidential election, Cyril celebrated flamboyantly in his off-duty clothes, which meant his sarong. At his house, which served as the informal party offices for the village, he and his friends spent the day of the election results engaged in serious drinking. In mid-afternoon, they spilled out into the road: they sang, they danced, Cyril climbed on a signboard at a road junction and harangued the crowd with a ribald speech. Finally, with his friends cheering, he tucked his sarong into his underpants and danced down the street in an impersonation of the failed opposition candidate in the role of a demon.

A couple of months later, when his party won an extension to their parliamentary majority in a contentious referendum, Cyril shed what few inhibitions he still had. This time he dropped his sarong altogether and danced down the street in his underpants.

As they say in Sri Lanka: what to do? As a witness to the first of these scandals, and an audience as friends excitedly whispered to me about the second, I was a fledgling ethnographer with a problem. Empirically, the political was an inescapable feature of the social landscape in which I was carrying out research. Put simply, it dominated everyday life in this corner of Sri Lanka in the early 1980s. Theoretically, I had no obviously adequate language with which to capture the exuberance and unboundedness of a moment like this. I address the inadequacies of the available theoretical languages – the by-then almost moribund tradition of classic political anthropology and the emerging wave of resistance studies – in the next chapter. Here I want merely to register my problem twenty years ago, because this book is the late product of a long coming to terms with the questions raised by Cyril's exhibition: questions about the political and questions about the potential role of anthropology in understanding the political.

Intellectually, it all started for me in Sri Lanka, and some of the examples that follow come from there, but in order to make sense of these examples I have had to look further afield. My period of looking has, of course, coincided with a wave of growing interest in other people's politics. This interest has shown itself in fruitful interdisciplinary conversation between anthropologists, sociologists, historians, political theorists, and those political scientists not trapped in the parochialism and formalism that have so disfigured the academic understanding of the political. Rather too much of this conversation has probably been provoked by the spectacle of political violence – the other unresolved problem I brought back from my first Sri Lankan fieldwork – and not quite enough by issues of poverty, of representation, and of the close relationship between the political structures of a postcolonial modernity and the attendant contours of social hope. Many of my examples are taken from India, and derive in part from the conversations I have had, not as an anthropologist, but as a regional specialist talking to friends from Delhi, Kolkata, Dhaka, and Kathmandu. In the years I have worked on these themes I have, though, also engaged with colleagues working in Europe, Africa, the Middle East, Latin America, and various outposts of the post-socialist world. Some of their concerns run throughout the book, but I engage them most directly in the concluding chapter, where I try to sketch out the themes I see as central to the newly emerging anthropology of the political.

Politics and Culture

This is also a book about politics and culture. At the very first – still in Sri Lanka ruminating on my puzzle – I thought my problems required nothing more than a case for including a cultural dimension in our understanding of politics. But as I worked on the themes I have explored in this book, I realized it was more complex and more important than that. In the past twenty years, the abstractions labelled 'politics' and 'culture' have had a curiously close relationship in anthropology. The so-called 'politics

5

of culture' – the self-consciousness about needing, having, and protecting one's culture, found in arguments on nationalism and multiculturalism – has undermined innocent anthropological references to culture and cultures. But, equally, the recognition that politics always happens in a culturally inflected way also undermines the naïve formalism found in a great deal of political science, not to mention much of the earlier work done in political anthropology.

This book, then, concerns the way in which the politicization of culture has destabilized anthropologists' assumptions about cultural difference, and the language we use to talk about it. But it also concerns the way politics operates in different cultural and historical contexts, and the need for anthropologists to distance themselves from the reductionist models of the political which dominate much academic writing. Of course these issues have taken on new significance since the collapse of the twin towers in September 2001. Suddenly the politics of cultural difference is high on everyone's intellectual agenda. In this context we might expect anthropological accounts of other people's politics to command a special authority in public discussion. On the whole, though, they do not, and popular understandings of the politics of cultural difference have been dominated by models of quite remarkable crudity.

Given the sheer unexpectedness of the events of September 11, it was extraordinary how many commentators, both academic and journalistic, claimed to have seen it coming all along. The version of 'we-told-you-so', most often heard in the mainstream media referred back to an article by a Harvard political scientist, Samuel Huntington, published in *Foreign Affairs* in 1993. Taking for his title a phrase from the historian of Islam, Bernard Lewis, Huntington spoke of a new world where conflict would not be primarily ideological or political-economic, but cultural: a world where we could expect (it was claimed with hindsight) more events like those in Manhattan on September 11, because what motivated those events was what had motivated both sides in the war in former Yugoslavia, and would motivate states and individuals in increasing numbers in the future: it was 'the clash of civilizations' (Huntington 1993).

Almost from its publication, critics have been lining up to point out the inevitable empirical weaknesses in Huntington's breezily confident mapping of the world's recent conflicts, and there seems little point in rehearsing the familiar contradictions and counter-factuals. (What about Northern Ireland? Iran and Iraq? Are Hindus and Buddhists in Sri Lanka members of two civilizations or one? And so on.) One reason for taking Huntington seriously is that, in providing a simple, somehow intuitively 'right', explanatory grid for making sense of a suddenly rather scary world, there is a real chance that his essay could be one of the most striking social scientific examples yet of Robert Merton's notion of the 'self-fulfilling prophecy' (Merton 1957 [1937]). If enough members of the foreign policy crowd, in Washington, London, Paris, or Berlin, believe that the world really is destined to split along 'civilizational' lines, then the likelihood is that they will act in ways that exacerbate, assume, and perhaps eventually *create* something like one of Huntington's 'cultural fault-lines'. Which is exactly what we have had to endure in recent years.

So critics need to do more than find fault at the level of detail: they also need to show, somehow, that there are other ways of rendering our world intelligible. One purpose of this book is to map out an approach to understanding other people's politics, which does not deny the real differences in values and history that animate political agents in different parts of the world, but equally does not presume that those differences are deeper or harder to reconcile than they may actually be. This is the second reason for starting with Huntington. His central hypothesis is stark and clear. In the new world we are entering: 'The great divisions among humankind and the dominating source of conflict will be *cultural*' (Huntington 1993: 22, my emphasis). Although, as I shall explain later in this chapter, the very idea of 'culture' has become the object of some suspicion in anthropology in recent years, nevertheless if anthropologists have any academic business which is properly theirs, it is the business of cultural difference. And so, if any academic discipline should come into its own in a world where 'culture' appears to lie behind more and more conflicts, then it should be anthropology.

At the heart of Huntington's argument lies a set of assumptions about culture, values, and the possibility of translation, and much of my argument in the first half of this book will concern, broadly speaking, issues of translation. For Huntington, cultural differences can be bundled up into 'civilizational' differences, with 'civilization' defined as 'the broadest level of cultural identity people have short of that which distinguishes humans from other species' (Huntington 1993: 24). Differences between civilizations are 'basic':

The people of different civilizations have different views on the relations between God and man, the individual and the group, the citizen and the state, parents and children, husband and wife, as well as differing views of the relative importance of rights and responsibilities, liberty and authority, equality and hierarchy. These differences are the product of centuries. They will not soon disappear. They are far more fundamental than differences among political ideologies and political regimes. (Huntington 1993: 25)

Huntington is not, then, arguing for complete incommensurability, for radically different vocabularies to describe 'individual', 'group', 'citizen', 'state', etc. He is arguing for different understandings of the 'relations between' these terms, understandings which are 'fundamental' because the product of long histories. He continues:

V. S. Naipaul has argued that Western civilization is the 'universal civilization' that 'fits all men'. At a superficial level much of Western culture has indeed permeated the rest of the world. At a more basic level, however, Western concepts differ fundamentally from those prevalent in other civilizations. Western ideas of individualism, liberalism, constitutionalism, human rights, equality, liberty, the rule of law, democracy, free markets, the separation of church and state, often have little resonance in Islamic, Confucian, Japanese, Hindu, Buddhist or Orthodox cultures. (Huntington 1993: 40)

Here it is the very 'concepts' which are said to differ, and 'Western ideas' are said to have 'little resonance' in other cultures.

This suggestion would seem to fit with two different strands of academic thought, one rather old and conventional, one more recent and apparently radical. In anthropology, at least since the 1960s, it has been widely argued that people in different cultures have radically different ideas about what it is to be a person, about the relationship between individual and collectivity, about the significance of differences of gender or age (e.g., Carrithers *et al.* 1985; Strathern 1988). In India, where many of my examples originate, society was described by an earlier generation of anthropologists as essentially hierarchical rather than egalitarian, and social relations were said to be oriented to the social whole rather than to the (mostly unacknowledged) individual (Dumont 1980). The other, more recent and radical, argument which echoes this part of Huntington's case focuses on the alleged universality of liberal principles. The 'universal' subject of post-Enlightenment political theory, we have been repeatedly told in recent years, is not universal at all – 'he' is gendered, white, European, heterosexual – and the appeal to universalism conceals the way in which marks of culture, race, gender, class, all work to exclude certain people from power. In this case, that academic grouping which Richard Rorty (Rorty 1998) has recently labelled the 'cultural left' finds itself singing in uneasy harmony with the hard-nosed pronouncements of the foreign policy hawks.

Meanwhile, other voices intrude on the debate. Lee Kuan Yew, fomer Prime Minister of Singapore, is quite clear about how little resonance Western political values have in Asia. Lee has spoken of 'the fundamental difference between Western concepts of society and government and East Asian concepts', while his Foreign Minister has warned that 'universal recognition of the ideal of human rights can be harmful if universalism is used to deny or mask the reality of diversity' (both cited in Sen 1997: 9, 13). Lee's views, like those of the equally authoritarian former Malaysian Prime Minister Mahathir, and the official ideologues of the

People's Republic of China, have been the subject of much debate and academic hand-wringing (see Bauer and Bell 1999). But probably the most compelling reason to treat the 'Asian values' argument with suspicion is the strong odour of *realpolitik* which accompanies it. Popular movements in Indonesia, the Philippines, and Myanmar, not to mention China itself in 1989, have all made strategic use of the rhetoric of democracy and rights; authoritarian rulers like Lee challenge the 'authenticity' of such rhetoric from below, but are happy to accommodate themselves to other, equally 'Western', political constructs, not least the very idea of the nation-state itself. The issue of translation and translatability is, to put it mildly, politically inflected.

Yet there is another way in which we might interpret the mystifying plausibility of Huntington's argument, and it is one that introduces a central theme of this book. The historic moment of 'The clash of civilizations' came immediately after the fall of the Berlin Wall, as other conservative ideologues celebrated the final triumph of liberalism and the 'end of history'. Functionalists on the left argued that this position was unsustainable. Put crudely, it could be argued that America, as the sole triumphant super-power, needed a new enemy and needed it badly. For generations, the American political imaginary had been grounded in the Manichean divide of Cold War anti-communism. In the words of one American icon, Marlon Brando, in *The Wild One* in answer to the question 'What are you rebelling against?' – 'What have you got?' It could be argued that there is nothing especially American in this. Earlier in the century, the German political philosopher Carl Schmitt argued that at the very heart of the political lay the distinction between friend and enemy (Schmitt 1996 [1932]): it followed that the liberal project, forever oriented to the reasonable resolution of political differences, would founder on its own contradictions. The new Manicheans, whose war on terror is also a war on the liberalism it purports to defend, are fuelled by the politics of the friend/enemy distinction, their practice one more manifestation of the agonistic heart of the political.

Schmitt, an unrepentant supporter of the Nazi regime, drew some pretty unsavoury conclusions from his diagnosis, but others have recently attempted to think creatively about lessons that can be learnt from Schmitt's critique of liberalism.[2] I would like to extend some of them to the practice of an anthropology of politics. If we are living in an era in which public discourse is dominated by the rhetoric of 'us' and 'them', civilization or barbarism, then anthropology itself may act as a kind of counter-politics, its promise to understand rather than condemn the Other, permanently and productively at odds with the political rhetoric of absolute incommensurability. In a recent speech, in which he presented himself as a humble commentator on the text of the Koran, Tony Blair gave the Huntington formula a new tweak:

This is not a clash between civilisations. It is a clash about civilisation. It is the age-old battle between progress and reaction, between those who embrace and see opportunity in the modern world and those who reject its existence; between optimism and hope on the one hand; and pessimism and fear on the other.[3]

I disagree profoundly with every aspect of this formulation. In this 'age-old battle', there is only one place for an an anthropologist with a social conscience: down there in the details of people's everyday lives, sympathetically pointing out the many ways the world does not readily divide into those with, and those without, 'civilization'.

Translation and the Problem of Culture

This has, as I have indicated, been a long journey for me. My first moment of revelation concerned not the possession or lack of civilization, nor even

---

[2] I develop these points later in the book, and return to them in the conclusion. My own thinking has been influenced by some, though by no means all, of Chantal Mouffe's reading of Schmitt (Mouffe 2000). For a salutary reminder of Schmitt's appalling personal politics see Lilla's usefully caustic assessment (Lilla 2001: 49–76).

[3] Tony Blair, Speech to the Foreign Policy Centre, 21 March 2006, full text accessed at http://politics.guardian.co.uk/iraq/story/0,,1736105,00.html, 24 May 2006.

cultural barriers to translation, but rather the translation, or appropriation, of the very notion of 'culture' itself. I have described this moment
before (Spencer 1990c), but it was so striking, and its implications so
important for my own understanding of the term 'culture', that I will
here rehearse my earlier description. This all happened in 1983, in a village in central Sri Lanka where I had been conducting anthropological
fieldwork for the past eighteen months. At a ceremony to mark my departure, a local schoolteacher gave a speech, setting out for his audience what
I would do when I returned to Britain. I was to write a book, he said,
about 'Sinhala culture', and this would show that Sinhala culture was
the best culture in the world. I was nonplussed: 'culture' was the 'thing'
I was supposed to be describing, not something on which 'they' were
expected to have a view. (If this sounds a little naïve on my part, so
be it.)

This was, of course, a classic moment of ethnographic reflexivity. I had
discovered no more than the inescapable fact that social researchers do
not exist somewhere 'outside' their field of study: they are part of the field
too. What I wrote about 'their' culture could have real implications for
them, and for me. It was thus a moment of rediscovered coevality – to use
Johannes Fabian's (1983) expression. Both the schoolteacher and I were
living in a shared social and political world, and both of us were using at
least some of the same intellectual materials to make sense of it. His sense
of 'culture' was, it was true, more of a 'high culture' sense than my own
fieldworker's version, which at that stage in my career owed most to the
likes of Clifford Geertz and Marshall Sahlins (Geertz 1973; Sahlins 1976).
But, as I reflected on this moment, I soon recognized the shared history
of the concept. The schoolteacher's culture was a 'national culture', it was
special, it had its unique character, it was the particular property of a
special group of people – Sinhala people. So, too, the notion of 'culture'
employed by American cultural anthropologists could be traced back –
via its configurationalist manifestation in the 1930s and 1940s – to the
founding father, Franz Boas. From him it was a short step to the German

romantic writers like Fichte, Humboldt, and especially Herder who had first articulated the vision of a world of nations, each with its characteristic 'spirit' or *geist*, which needed to be nurtured in its characteristic way: 'culture' was both the medium for, and the product of, that process of nurturing the distinctive spirit of a group of people.

Other anthropologists in other places were noticing the same problem, notably Michael Herzfeld, researching on the history of folklore in Greece, and Richard Handler, who had set out to write an ethnography of Quebecois nationalism 'as a cultural system', only to discover his master concept was already part of his ethnographic problem, and thus ruled out from being part of his theoretical solution (Herzfeld 1986; Handler 1988). Unease at culture's shared intellectual lineage with nationalism was compounded by a second line of critique. This could be traced to Edward Said's swingeing attack on European representations of 'the East', representations which, he charged, fixed the Other in a discourse of ahistorical stereotypes. At the end of *Orientalism* he asked a question: 'Is the notion of a distinct culture (or race, or religion, or civilization) a useful one, or does it always get involved either in self-congratulation (when one discusses one's own) or hostility and aggression (when one discusses the 'other')?' (Said 1978: 325). In other words, academic depictions of a world of different cultures cannot easily escape the evaluative implications of the term. In response to Said, the critic James Clifford wrote of the need for some way of addressing culture's 'differential and relativist functions' while avoiding 'the positing of cosmopolitan essences and human common denominators' (Clifford 1988: 274–5). (It was the 1980s: 'difference', in its many spellings, was 'in', and any hint of the universal was 'out'.) But, as Clifford had written elsewhere in the same collection: 'Culture is a deeply compromised idea I cannot yet do without' (Clifford 1988: 10). By the early 1990s, though, even if the tensions identified by Clifford remained far from resolved, a new generation of anthropologists had learned to avoid the 'billiard ball' vision of a world of bounded, internally homogeneous 'cultures'.

What then was the alternative? And how do we deal with the issue of translation? After all, many of the fiercest critics of 'essentialism', as they discerned it in previous anthropology, were equally fiercely committed to a recognition of potentially radical cultural difference. One alternative was to employ other words altogether to do the work we might have expected of 'culture' – like the Foucaultian use of 'discourse' (Abu Lughod 1991). Another was to attempt to model the dynamic, unbounded movement of cultural stuff in a world of increasingly globalized cultural production and reproduction (Hannerz 1987; Appadurai 1990). A third was to remind younger readers that, in fact, a concern with historical contingency and internal complexity was at the very heart of anthropological arguments in the 1930s, and the cliché of cultures as timeless, bounded entities was probably never really believed in by anyone (Sahlins 1999). A fourth was to drop the term 'culture', but instead configure it as the 'local', which denoted the cultural stuff employed in the process of resisting (usually), or appropriating (occasionally), the forces of global capital and Euroaomerican modernity. All of these reappear, sometimes in heavy disguise, in chapter three, which revisits late colonial interpretations of new institutions in unexpected cultural contexts.

But what of translation? There is a straightforward question to be answered in Huntington's hypothesis: does the language of Western politics 'translate' into other cultural contexts? Or, as the examples I opened with make clear, not so much *does* it translate, but rather, *how* does it translate in any particular context? What possibilities emerge, what predicaments must be confronted?

Identifying the Political

'MGR is a god; MGR is a king; MGR is my leader' (Dickey 1993: 351). In one of the foundational texts of political anthropology, Meyer Fortes and Edward Evans-Pritchard had argued that 'A comparative study of political systems has to be on an abstract plane where social processes are stripped of their cultural idiom and are reduced to functional terms' (Fortes and Evans-Pritchard 1940: 3). Sara Dickey's quote from a supporter of the South Indian movie star-politician M. G. Ramachandram (of whom more in chapter two) indicates what might be lost if we insist on excluding local meanings from our definition of the political.

If culture is one of my themes, so too is politics. It is an equally complex term. If we look at the English-language history of the notion of 'politics', we find two broad strands. One links politics to government, and especially the state: 'The science and art of government; the science dealing with the form, organization, and administration of a state or part of one, and with the regulation of its relations with other states' (*OED*, s.v. politic B.3 *pl.*). The other emphasizes a certain mode of conduct, either conceived in a positive light – 'judicious, expedient, skilfully contrived' – or more negatively, 'scheming, crafty, cunning' (*OED*, s.v. politic A.2). Neither of these, it seems to me, quite comes to terms with Cyril's underpants, or with any of the examples of South Asian political life that follow in the next chapter. The politics I encountered in Sri Lanka, and which I want to talk about in this book, is a politics of semiotic excess, of transgression, of occasional violence, of humour and entertainment, love and fear.

The politics of classic political anthropology, as I shall show in the next chapter, leaned towards the second strand – politics as calculated instrumentality – and away from the first, not least in order to show that we can talk of politics and the political in societies with differing kinds of state or with no state at all. The result was spectacularly successful in the short run – witness, from a classic of its time, F. G. Bailey's fast-cuts between an American mafia trial, a British political memoir, and his own field material from an Indian village (Bailey 1969) – but predictably banal and un-anthropological in the long run. It was banal because, in the end, it all got to look very much the same. And if the game allows us to see University committees and Indian villages as but variants on a single theme of political strategizing, this may make the committees mildly more interesting, for a time at least, but only by making the villages a great deal less interesting, immediately.

The politics-as-politicking approach was problematic for another reason. As we have seen, its strongest rationale was the extension of the idea of the political to contexts in which something like the modern European state was either absent altogether, or at least quite distant. But the claim that there were 'societies without states' was questionable enough in the late colonial era of the 1930s, and became quite nonsensical in the era of decolonization. Now, though, even the most marginalized and stereotypically 'primitive' groups of people are used to presenting themselves as 'nations' seeking recognition from the larger state in which they find themselves living. No one is entirely free from the idea of the state, although how analytically helpful that idea actually is is more of an open question.

I devote two central chapters to the anthropology of the state. In the first of these I review recent attempts to see beyond the fictions of the state-as-idea or symbol. In the second I use the issue of violence as a way of opening out a rather different discussion about the state. The third critical moment in my fieldwork – eight months after Cyril's performance and three before the schoolteacher's speech – occurred in July 1983. An attack on government soldiers by Tamil separatists near the northern city of Jaffna was followed by a week of violence against the Tamil minority in the south of the country: houses were torched, shops looted, and people caught by the perpetrators were beaten and, in some cases, killed. Although the crude body-count has been far higher at many points in the civil war that followed these events, the 1983 violence has a special significance in Sri Lankan history. It has also been the subject of much analysis, by anthropologists and other social scientists. In my discussion here I turn away from earlier anthropological work, with its focus on victims (Daniel 1996), or its search for some chimerical cultural logic at work in the violence (Kapferer 1988), and insist instead on the irreducibly *political* dimension of the events of July 1983 (not to mention most of the violence in the years that followed). In chapter six I connect this point to some important recent arguments about violence and the distribution of sovereignty in the postcolonial world.

But in describing the 1983 violence as irreducibly political, I am not merely saying that this violence was predominantly carried out by agents of a political party, with the connivance of police and other officials. That is true enough, but I am also pointing to an important dimension of the political. I have already hinted at this in referring to its unboundedness, its capacity to spill out of the safe institutional boundaries in which it is supposedly contained by modern states. Put simply, the political is productive as well as destructive. Violence is an obvious mark of destruction, although it often creates the possibility for new or altered forms of subjectivity and solidarity in its wake. The forms of power and critique created within the institutions of modern mass politics have a similarly ambivalent capacity. Many of the familiar shapes of the social order may be swept away – or so some believe – even as new forms of solidarity, the 'us' and 'them' of representative democracy, are produced or strengthened. In chapter four I concentrate on the performative dimension of mass democracy, and show how self-conscious ideas about the political represent an attempt to contain and control the agonistic energies unleashed in electoral politics. In chapter seven I challenge the self-evidences of multicultural theory, and try to show how ethnic (or other) solidarities are the consequences, rather than the causes, of political competition.

There are two aspects of my version of the political which I hope differentiate my argument from earlier traditions of political anthropology. One is the attempt to work with an expansive definition of the political, a definition which gives as much weight to the expressive and performative aspects of politics as to the instrumental. The other is the dynamic force of the political. In this argument 'politics' and 'culture' are not two discrete 'things', brought together in a controlled interaction. Analytically they can be better treated as two perspectives on a single dynamic process. The central mystery of the process is the promise of democracy – 'it ought to be ordinary people . . and not extraordinary people who rule' – which John Dunn has recently described as at once obvious but also 'tantalizingly strange and implausible' (Dunn 1992: v). This book seeks to capture some of this sense of strangeness and implausibility by using anthropological evidence to defamiliarize assumptions usually treated as self-evident in the study of modern politics. The next chapter starts to put some flesh on this, so-far over-abstract, notion of the political.

TWO

Locating the Political

Introduction

In 1984 the Tamil movie star and politician, M. G. Ramachandram, was paralysed by a stroke. For three years he lived on in a Brooklyn hospital room, his followers celebrating the miracle of the 'thrice-born' leader's survival. Finally in 1987 the end came. M. S. S. Pandian uses what followed to introduce his short monograph on MGR:

Perhaps the best way to begin the incomparable success story of Marudur Gopalamenon Ramachandram (popularly known as MGR) and his politics, is to begin with his funeral . . . No less than two million people, including several who had travelled long distances from remote villages, formed MGR's rather long funeral procession. In other places, people who could not attend the actual funeral organized mock 'funerals' in which images of MGR were taken out in procession and buried with full ritual. Countless young men tonsured their heads, a Hindu ritual usually performed when someone of the family dies. Thirty-one of his desolate followers, unable to contain their grief, committed suicide. (Pandian 1992: 17)

Two million mourners, thirty-one suicides: MGR's life has been mapped out in such apparently surreal statistics: in 1967, when a fellow actor shot him, 50,000 fans gathered at the hospital where he was treated. When he suffered his stroke in 1984, 'At least twenty-two people immolated themselves, or cut off their limbs, fingers or toes as offerings to various deities, praying for the ailing leader's life.' During this last illness, 27,000 new roadside shrines were constructed in Tamil Nadu (Pandian 1992: 18).

The roads in the north-eastern state of Bihar have also been witness to some interesting political phenomena, notably the arrest of the BJP leader A. K. Advani on his theatrical progression towards the Babri Masjid mosque in Ayodhya in 1990. The Chief Minister for Bihar at the time was Laloo Prasad Yadav. Since 1997, Prasad has been jailed at least five times in the judicial fall-out from his larger-than-life administration of the state. In November 2001 he was ordered to surrender to the court in Ranchi. Here, from the Indian magazine *Frontline*, is an account of Laloo's trip to court:

Laloo Prasad arrived in Ranchi with fanfare, travelling on a motorized chariot which he called Sadbhavna rath. The journey was more than anything a political show. The RJD supremo's entourage consisted of hundreds of horses, camels, elephants and a music band. Supporters presented him with a sword as he travelled in his air-conditioned rath, which was escorted by a kilometres-long cavalcade. Party workers chanted slogans such as: 'Laloo Yadav mat ghabrana, tere peechee sara zamana (Don't worry Laloo Yadav, the entire people are behind you).' Laloo Prasad stopped en route at Biharsgarif to offer chaddar (a length of holy cloth) at the tomb of the Sufi saint Makhdom Baba. The cavalcade virtually laid siege to the highway leading to Ranchi. (Chaudhuri 2001)

Horses, camels, elephants: I guess we're not in Kansas any more. Laloo's career has been built upon his position as a member of a numerically powerful group, the Yadavs, who have been active within the politicization of the so-called Backward Classes since the 1970s. When the LSE anthropologist Lucia Michelutti carried out fieldwork with Yadavs in Uttar Pradesh a few years ago, she was told that they were a 'martial race', and 'by caste "natural" politicians':

1 'We are a caste of politicians' (All India Yadav Mahasabha Convention, 1999)

Informants explain their predisposition to succeed in the political game as 'innate'. They said that 'they learn it in the womb' (*pet se sikhte hai*) and that they were born to be politicians. They also invoked the 'womb' metaphor when they answered my queries about apprenticeship, especially in relation to activities related to the cow-herding profession. (Michelutti 2004: 46)[1]

Yadavs are good, they say, at 'doing politics'.

Not everyone, though, is quite so happy with this version of the *dharma* of the politician. In West Bengal, another LSE anthropologist, Arild Ruud, encountered a rather different valuation of the political. In the opening months of his fieldwork, people persistently berated him on the topic of 'politics':

---

[1]   Yadavs were 'traditionally' cowherds and farmers.

One term that was often used is 'dirty' (*nungra*). Politics was referred to as being dirty, meaning unprincipled, as something unsavoury that morally upright people would not touch, a sullied game of bargaining and dishonesty. Another term that was frequently employed to describe this foul game was 'disturbance' (*gandagol*). Politics, it was held, represented a continuous social disturbance that caused unease, brought disharmony to society, and ruined its elaborate design and calm stability. The reason for this, I was told, was that politics thrived on instances of trouble, or 'rows' (*jhamela*). These could be outright fist-fights (*maramari*), or abusive exchanges (*galagali*), drawn-out quarrels (*jhagra*), or just general animosity and hostility (*hingsa*). (Ruud 2001: 116)

In the essay from which this is taken, Ruud goes on to explore the local construction of politics as dirty work, within the framework of what he calls the 'Indianization' of political institutions. Although he spends some time trying to work out why so many people turned up for an apparently pointless and rather dull village political meeting, Ruud does not comment on the very frequency with which people told him about the unsavouriness of local politics, the apparent enthusiasm with which they reported on the moral failings of political leaders. Reading between the lines, my sense is that these Bengali villagers, like people across the subcontinent, were at once appalled and fascinated by the workings of the political. What grips them at one level is the sheer melodrama of it all, the ostentatiously performed agonism of the exchanges between political opponents, as well as the symbolic excess of South Asia's magical realist politicians – elephants and camels on the road to jail.

The central argument of this book concerns the domain of the political. In postcolonial South Asia, the political has emerged as a complex field of social practices, moral judgements, and imaginative possibilities. Although recent ethnography gives us a much fuller and better sense of what ordinary men and women make of politics and the political, our theoretical apparatus has been slow to catch up with the richness and diversity of the phenomena to be explained. This chapter attempts to

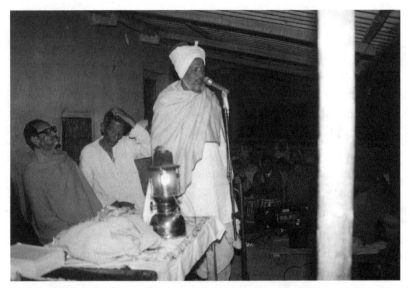

2 The 'dirty work' of politics (village meeting, West Bengal)

diagnose the problem posed by the political, looking at two very different attempts to locate and analyse it. The first is the instrumental understanding of politics and the political, found in classic political anthropology, as well as a great deal of political science. This, in its strongest versions, is a politics without values. The second attempt, which was partly constituted in a reaction to narrow interpretations of the political, is found in historical and ethnographic work on the issue of resistance. Here I will narrow my focus to one particular strand of that work – that produced by the Subaltern Studies group of historians and theorists from the 1980s onward. I concentrate in particular on the programmatic statements of the group's senior theorist Ranajit Guha. While this work redresses the imaginative failings of instrumentalist political science, it also deliberately excludes the state from the domain of authentic politics. Some of the problems this creates for our understanding of politics in the here and now will be explored further in later chapters.

Nepal: Dissent in a Lordly Idiom

In 1984, the anthropologist Richard Burghart travelled to Nepal on a project to investigate attitudes to drinking water and hygiene. He did indeed investigate attitudes to drinking water, writing one classic paper on the development expert's *lack* of agency on the way (Burghart 1993). But he also became increasingly fascinated by events in the country at large. The 1980s were a decade of profound unease in the Nepali polity. The country, which was never colonized but which had to survive in the shadow of British colonial power for many years, proudly proclaimed itself the world's only surviving Hindu monarchy. After a brief flirtation with party politics in the 1950s, King Mahendra dismissed the elected government in 1960 and promulgated a new constitution in 1962. Under this constitution, the King continued to rule, but was advised by an assembly or *panchayat*, which was part elected, part appointed. Crucially, though, political parties were forbidden, because, as sectional expressions of private interest, they were alien to the distinctive moral ethos of the Nepali polity, in which the collective welfare of all was embodied in the singular person of the King.

During Burghart's fieldwork, dissatisfaction with the status quo built up and expressed itself in a series of public confrontations with the authorities. In December 1984 teachers went on a token strike, protesting at the erosion of their salary levels. In early 1985, their demands were taken up by student groups and banned political parties. More strikes, protests, and arrests followed in an atmosphere of mounting crisis until, in June 1985, the country was shocked by a set of explosions in symbolically potent sites (in front of the assembly building and the royal palace as well as in various provincial towns). The strikers immediately backed down in a gesture of national unity. In 1990, though, similar pressures for reform built up, and this time the King was forced to concede ground to the protestors, abolishing the system of '*panchayat* democracy' which had been in place since 1962 and clearing the ground for open elections the following year.

Inspired by the events in Nepal at the time, Burghart wrote a paper in 1991, analysing the protests of 1984–5 as a product of a set of radically different ideas about power, agency, authority, and criticism, ideas summed up in his notion of a 'lordly political culture':

To summarize, the strike proceeded in three stages. The lord is the mental agent, commanding the instruments who are likened to limbs of his body. Should the instruments find their lord negligent or overbearing, they inform him that there is some grievance that arises not from their own critical minds, but from force of circumstances . . . The workforce honour their lord by remaining part of the body politic and attributing agency to their master. The benevolent lord shows his sense of responsibility by enquiring into the grief-provoking 'circumstances'. At this stage in the micro-polity of the organization there is still only one mind, that of the lord, but the lord is unable to co-ordinate and command the instruments of his rule. The body politic exists, but does not function. The ruled show to the ruler that without their support he lacks the means of rule. (Burghart 1996: 316)

In concrete terms, this meant, for example, that the first stage of the strike was relatively brief. Teachers turned up to work, but wore black armbands, and kept silent in their classes – their inaction a deliberate sign to the lord of the ailment in the collective body. In the words of one of Burghart's informants, 'They inform management that they do this not of their will (*man*) but by force of circumstances (*majburi*)' (Burghart 1996: 310).

Burghart's point in this essay is to show the oblique forms which political criticism takes in a cultural context in which agency is invested in the lord – in this case the King – and in which passivity, not activity, becomes the most culturally coherent medium for expressing dissatisfaction with current circumstances. The nuances of the lordly idiom are further explored in the paper on drinking water, which charts his ham-fisted attempts to help a group of poor Cobblers purify their well: in this case, the Cobblers, through their considered passivity, forced the ethnographer into the lorldly position of expert and agent, with the responsibility to clean the well (Burghart 1993). (Needless to say, the ethnographer's efforts end in glorious failure.) The broader understanding of this lordly idiom comes from Burghart's earlier work on kingship, hierarchy, and culture, but the essay on the Cobblers' well and the essay on political criticism form a perfect pair, each illuminating the other. Crucially, understanding the forms of political criticism in the mid-1980s was an integral part of a longer career dedicated to the analysis of South Asian societies as culturally complex phenomena, in which Burghart explored an increasingly reflexive attitude to the moments of collusion and misapprehension that link anthropologists to the people they work with.

Burghart's work on political culture in Nepal was incomplete at the time of his tragic death in 1994. Many of its themes, though, are taken up in more recent work by the American anthropologist Vincanne Adams. In a recent ethnography (Adams 1998), she has analysed the events of 1990, concentrating especially on the role of medical professionals as the intellectual and political vanguard of the democratic revolution in Nepal. Where Burghart tries to draw the reader into an altogether alien political idiom, in which agency is vested in the King and protest is perforce oblique in its manifestations, Adams' doctors speak with great clarity on themes which appear on the surface to be far more familiar: the self-evident political virtues of democracy, science, and scientific truth. Working from interviews conducted a few years after the crucial events, she reconstructs the central role of the doctors in the upheavals of 1990. Her problem – which obviously owes much to the post-Foucaultian mood in American academic attitudes to modernity – is to explain how it is that Western medicine and Western science came to be seen as unproblematically progressive forces for postcolonial radicals like the Nepali doctors. In other words, it is liberal democracy and scientific objectivity, in their Nepali expression, which serve as the 'Other' which requires contextualization and explanation in Adams' account.

The doctors' action itself started by echoing the earlier teachers' protest, as analysed by Burghart: a two-hour token strike of hospital doctors, protesting at government brutality to demonstrators, accompanied by the wearing of symbolic black armbands. Then as the unrest in the country intensified, medical professionals increasingly used their professional authority as a strategic resource in the protests: making speeches from public platforms, and using the hospitals as bases of protest. In one extraordinary scene, a group of doctors are attempting to make their way across town during a huge anti-govenment demonstration, despite the fact that all official-looking vehicles are potential objects of attack:

They had made it no closer than the northern outskirts of town . . when their bus was attacked by protestors. Hands filled with stones and bricks, the people began coming towards them. Those inside were fearful that the bus would be overturned by the crowd. Then one doctor stood up to call to the crowd at the exit door, and a protestor outside recognized the doctors and nurses by their white coats – clearly on their way to the Tundikhel where they would join the crowd in support of the movement. He yelled, 'It is the doctors!' The people dropped their stones and bricks and slowly they moved towards the bus, and to the astonishment of the passengers within they began to kiss it. (Adams 1998: 127–8)

For the doctors themselves, their protests were an extension of their professional responsibilities. In the words of one prominent doctor, recalling a conversation with the then Minister of Health:

We are voicing . . . we are protesting against this arrest and treatment of our colleagues, aginst the killing of people. This is totally a non-political issue. This is against the killing of innocent people who have done nothing but were killed. We are talking about human rights violations, the brutality of the police who entered the hospital and did violent things inside the hospital. (Adams 1998: 95)

What Adams eventually uncovers is an unresolved tension between universalist talk of rights and equality, and more local social idioms of connectedness, familiality, and moral duty, idioms which are recognizably part of the social universe described by Burghart. In the years building up to the 1990 protests, the everyday workings of the *panchayat* system – in which access to resources depended on activating social networks which linked the petitioner, through however many intermediaries, to the central figure of the King – became increasingly revalued as immoral or corrupt. The doctors epitomized a kind of social practice – that of Western biomedicine – which was thought to transcend the partialities of social connection and familial favouritism. To the extent that the everyday politics of social connection obstructed doctors' efforts to deliver adequate health care, then invoking the language of universal rights and equality – in short, the language of democracy – could be seen as a logical extension of their existing medical practice. After the revolution, though, when political parties started to act as possible conduits of resources, tensions started to appear. Were the doctors now just playing 'politics' like their corrupt predecessors? For many poorer members of society, 'democracy' had promised not just equality of standing before the law, or the possibility of participating in representative politics: it had also strongly implied equality of access to state resources. Not surprisingly, all subsequent compromises with this central promise, however objectively 'inevitable', could be seen as failings of democracy.[2]

Yet, as Adams shows, to participate in social networks, to look after members of your own family, to accept responsibility for a client who needs support, are all ways of action which could be perceived as distinctively Nepali (Adams 1998: 228–9). What emerges from this is an idea of 'politics' and 'the political' which is inherently unstable and morally fraught. In the words of one of her informants:

Let us take the example of a school. School is not for personal benefit. It is for everyone. [Lists different political parties.] It is for everyone's children. Here the parents also get involved. So school is a very pure organization. Medicine

---

[2] For more recent, and more detailed, reports on the curious fate of democracy in Nepal, see the various contributions to Gellner (2003), especially Millard's (2003) especially vivid account of local disenchantment in a remote area of the country.

should be the same. If politics is played here, it is going to spoil the school. This is why development and politics differ. This is why health and politics differ. It is like a river with two rivulets joining it. Democracy runs a country and for this a very powerful dam is needed, so that it cannot divert and go the wrong way. Due to lack of knowledge and poverty, it is easy for people to be bought, and they sell out. They sell their votes. A person is bought and sold for his vote. (Adams 1998: 194–5)

These examples from Nepal bring out a number of themes which will be explored later in this book. Obviously, both ethnographers are explicitly concerned with the cultural consequences of political modernity: Burghart in tracing the persistence and ubiquity of his lordly social idiom, Adams in stressing the cultural specificity of the 'universal' language of science, rights, and democracy. Both can be read as telling us something quite important about the difficulties of drawing bounds round 'the political': the practices and assumptions which structure the strikes and demonstrations, in Burghart's account of the mid-1980s, also structure his encounter with the Cobblers in his guise as visiting expert. The doctors who insisted their involvement in political protest was engendered by their impartial professional ethic then had to cope with their ongoing work in a world in which partiality – and the politics of partiality – were inescapable. Interestingly, and less obviously, both Burghart and Adams are concerned with issues of culture and authenticity. Adams' first ethnography, *Tigers of the Snow and Other Virtual Sherpas* (Adams 1996), invokes the extended metaphor of the mirror in order to address the complex interaction between Sherpa self-representations and the many powerful versions of Sherpa identity available from outsiders. Burghart's work, from the early 1980s until his death in 1994, was above all concerned with the complexities of translation – something, he insisted, which goes on as much *within* particular cultural settings as it does between them. I shall return to the issue of translation, and re-examine the supposed singularity of the modern in the chapters which follow.

India: The Spectre of the State

The material from Nepal in the 1980s has a special fascination because of the peculiar historical circumstances of that country. In particular, the idea and practice of democracy reappear with unusual freshness in Adams' ethnography. Elsewhere on the subcontinent, democracy remains a potent notion, even if its practices are now more than a little shop-worn. To find equivalents to Adams' ethnography of the coming of democracy, we would have to turn to the fieldworkers of the 1950s and 1960s – Bailey, Béteille, Fox – who charted the early impact of the inexorable arithmetic of electoral democracy upon local caste hierarchies (Bailey 1963; Béteille 1965; Fox 1969; see Gould 2003 for a recent survey of this work). Until recently, these themes retreated to the bottom of the ethnographic agenda, but the rise of the Hindu right in India, and the concomitant increase in ethnic and communal tension, have now brought forth a new wave of ethnographies of the political. These, though, look at politics and the state from a number of obvious and not-so-obvious perspectives.

In Benaras the wrestlers are clear on the virtues of discipline: the young Hindu men who wrestle in public, pride themselves on their regimens of bodily perfection. They are careful to eat properly, to exercise properly, to shit properly. According to their ethnographer, Joseph Alter, their rationale for these practices is a political one:

When reflecting on the nature of what it is they are doing, they often begin to talk about the political and moral climate of modern India. They are highly critical of the government's role in public welfare and policy. Wrestlers are also very critical of the character of modern Indian men, particularly young men, who are seen as preoccupied with sex, greed, and sensual gratification of all kinds. Senior wrestlers in Benaras would often point out and vocally criticize young men for sporting 'hippi-cut' hair styles, tight-fitting 'bush shirts', and snug polyester trousers. (Alter 1993: 56–7)

The corruption and decadence of modern Independent India is contrasted with the order and discipline of the old princely states, in which many wrestlers pursued their calling.[3]

Alter's wrestlers have a vision of a utopian India, in which the disciplined bodies of the wrestlers transcend the divisions of politics, caste, and community. Other wrestlers, though, have darker visions. In his recent book on the causes and consequences of religious violence in India, the psycho-analyst Sudhir Kakar describes his encounter with two 'riot captains' in urban Hyderabad. Both are wrestlers – one Hindu, one Muslim. Their relationship with the local state is a great deal less reflective than the Benaras wrestlers, as described by Alter. Much of their income comes from so-called 'land business' – acting as hired enforcers for the urban middle classes whose property interests are no longer adequately protected by the creaky machinery of the formal legal system – but their fame derives in large part from their role as fighters in the city's intermittent Hindu–Muslim clashes. A story about an older wrestler's retirement from street violence in the late 1970s provides a different twist to Alter's argument:

Since each one of us interprets the world from the limited view we have of it, Sufi Pehlwan too saw the deterioration of the country through his particular professional lens. The quality of food and thus the toughness of men's bodies had been steadily degenerating over the years. Bones had become brittle so that when one stabbed a person there was hardly any resistance to the knife

---

[3] Oddly, though, Alter insists on forcing the wrestlers' testimony into a somewhat strained Foucaultian mould. When the wrestlers lament the lack of discipline and order in the modern state and modern public life, Alter interprets this as a complaint against state technologies which, he claims they say, *make* docile bodies. To me, they seem to be saying it is the absence of discipline that is the problem, not the presence of state technologies. What, to this reader, looks like a call for a stronger state and a more vigorous sense of bodily discipline is turned, by Alter, into a rather predictable act of resistance *against* the Indian state. His examples in fact make most sense if re-interpreted not in terms of the Foucault of *Discipline and Punish* (1977), but in terms of 'late Foucault', and especially the writing on 'technologies of the self' (cf. Mahmood 2001; Laidlaw 2002).

blade which sliced through muscle, cartilage, and bone as if they were wet clay. Simply put, there was no longer any professional satisfaction to be obtained from a riot, and Sufi Pehlwan had turned to other, more challenging, if perhaps less exciting pursuits. (Kakar 1996: 82)

The moral and political order, for this man, is so decadent that even the communal rioting is not what it once was.

The wrestlers are urban men, and their viewpoint on the postcolonial state may be dismissed as too marginal for serious attention. Nevertheless, there is a strong chorus of moral lamentation for the ways of politics and the feebleness of the state, to be heard all over the subcontinent in one form or another. Nor are the wrestlers unique in the unexpected links they draw between the political order and the moral order, and between collective events and individual somatic distress.

Politics without Culture

All the examples so far have illuminated one or other facet of what we might understand as 'the political' in contemporary South Asia. The political encompasses the village meeting, the nasty local gossip about the backstage deals of local leaders, the lamentations of the wrestlers, but also the spectacular excesses of a Laloo or an MGR. In Sri Lanka in the early 1980s I encountered all of this. In purely entertainment terms, political rallies were the biggest shows in town, with speeches and singers and the helicopter touching down with the biggest of the big cheeses to attend. In the village where I conducted my fieldwork, people spoke of politics (*desapalanaya*) in terms very like Ruud's Bengali informants: as a dirty business, a source of trouble and moral disturbance. But the political, so construed, also stood as the ground against which other, more positive, images crystallized: the political rally was the quintessential setting for the enunciation of nationalist rhetoric, for speeches about the Sinhala people and their destiny as Guardian of the island of Lanka and protector of the heritage of the Buddha. As well as the pop singers and politicoes, there would always be a body of Buddhist monks on the platform at local rallies, lending the occasion a minimal sense of gravitas (Figure 4). The agonistic world of politics contained, within it, expressions of its own negation: the transcendence of division and interest signified, in their different ways, in the symbolism of the nation and the presence of the body (*sangha*) of Buddhist monks. For every instance of the political, there is at least one, if not more, mode of the anti-political.

There was something electric about Sri Lankan local politics in the early 1980s, a sense of excitement and unpredictability. Partly this was a result of the way in which national politics had become braided into the very fabric of local sociality: neighbours pursued neighbour-type disputes about chickens and buffaloes in the idiom of party political divisions. The politically connected prospered, the politically disconnected were persecuted. Eager lads attached themselves to minor local leaders, basking in their own ephemeral importance in the leader's retinue, and ever ready to throw their weight around when so required. Everyone discussed the doings of national politicians in first-name terms.

But electricity contains its dangers too. Violence was a real threat in local politics and, after I left, the capillaries of neighbourhood political divisions became the channels through which denunciations and counter-denunciations flowed as the island was swept by a wave of political terror. A radical group called the JVP targeted local agents of the ruling party; the powers-that-be in their retaliations sometimes identified whole categories, young men from particular castes or villages, and sometimes just picked on old enemies with much more particular scores to settle. The violence shocked and horrified my own closest informants when I spoke to them a few years later: this was not like our country, they told me, everything was turned upside down. And, as one told me, 'We don't do politics any more' (Spencer 2000).

What to do? (To repeat my earlier question.) It was the early 1980s, and there I was, an Anglo-Saxon empiricist committed to writing about what was there, and not what I would have liked to be there. Nothing had prepared me for my hosts' obsession with the political, and intellectually little came along during the 1980s in my lonely hunt for an appropriate intellectual toolkit. Let me start with the most obvious suspect: political anthropology. What was so wrong with what was called political anthropology in the late 1970s? A casual answer might simply be that it was boring, a subdiscipline that had run out of steam at some point in the early 1970s. Behind that rather jaundiced assessment lies one partial truth: that what made political anthropology less and less interesting was its propensity to strip away whatever was distinctive and interesting about any particular bit of politics in the first place, and *that* in turn was a consequence of the very way in which it had been defined. If the anthropological study of politics has to be 'on an abstract plane where social processes are stripped of their cultural idiom and are reduced to functional terms' (Fortes and Evans-Pritchard 1940: 3), its products are necessarily going to be somewhat smaller than life. No camels and elephants for them. The price of reducing something, as we all know, is reductionism, and that particular spectre has haunted political anthropology ever after.

Quite apart from its hostility to particular 'cultural idioms', political anthropology also evaded the moral dimension of the political:

I assume that individuals faced with a choice of action will commonly use such choice so as to gain power, that is to say they will seek recognition as social persons who have power; or, to use a different language, they will seek to gain access to office or the esteem of their fellows which may lead them to office. (Leach 1954: 10)

Edmund Leach's heuristic has a long provenance in Western social thought. One lineage leads back to Machiavelli's espousal of a cold-eyed realism in assessing human affairs: 'I shall set aside fantasies about rulers, then, and consider what happens in fact' (Machiavelli 1988: 54).[4] The

---

[4] The Machiavellian commitment to realism in political analysis still retains much of its potency, as I shall argue in the conclusion to this book.

other derives from that moment in the eighteenth century, magisterially analysed by Albert Hirschman (1977), when social thinkers started to separate the 'passions' from the 'interests', allowing their successors to posit a rational, calculating individual as the ontological basis, the axis of certainty, for the emerging human sciences. Which, needless to say, does not stop Leach's formula sounding quite a bit like the view from Bengal or Sri Lanka, where politics is indeed often seen as the zone of untrammelled individual interest. But there is a difference in tone: Leach, unlike Ruud's peasants, sees nothing corrupting or 'dirty', there is no 'disturbance', in his view of human action. Rather, 'a conscious or unconscious wish to gain power is a very general motive in human affairs' (Leach 1954: 10). Leach's urbane generalization somehow strips this kind of action of its power to disturb us. To seek power in some sense or other is an unremarkable course of action, true enough; but to seek power and nothing else, nakedly, in public, strikes many people as strange and rather disturbing. The effect of Leach's heuristic, and the tradition of thought he is speaking from, is to *naturalize* such conduct, to deprive it of its sense of moral danger and make it, instead, something banal and commonplace. Hirschman's marvellous essay is partly concerned to remind us of the tortuous path that eventually allowed social philosophers to claim a direct causal link between the pursuit of the personal interest and the moral improvement of the collectivity. The point is simple: such a link is far from self-evident, and the Bengali village reaction is a recurrent feature of people's encounter with the agonistic space of the political. A cluck of disapproval is perhaps the most common mode of the counter-political.

As political anthropology became routinized in the 1950s and 1960s it did so in the long and gloomy shadow cast by its big sister, political science. Looking back at the literature of that time, two aspects stand out. One, obviously enough, is the confident deployment of the cool language of dispassionate science: 'Ways of viewing the differences between political and other kinds of social relationships are neither right nor wrong but merely more or less useful for scientific purposes', as the political scientist David Easton (Easton 1959: 219) put it in a once-influential survey of political anthropology. Classic political anthropology was greatly concerned with definitions of its subject matter, formal models, and typologies. These may have had their use in marking out a certain territory for the new subdiscipline, but they also had one other effect: to pin down, and thus somehow *contain* the political. If the empirical – *and* moral *and* political – problem we are trying to analyse is in part the very uncontainability of the political, its tendency to overflow its banks and wash through all areas of social life, this stance is, to put it no stronger, unhelpful.

In the South Asian context, the major theme of political anthropologists in the 1960s was the 'great Indian faction'. In a curious historical conjunction, empiricist political anthropology met Eurocentric modernization theory to argue that factions and factionalism were the culturally specific form of political organization in South Asia (Hardiman 1982). One problem with this argument is not that there are no factions, or patron–client ties, or vertical alliances in South Asian politics; the problem is, rather, how little the analysis of such phenomena tells us about the larger issues of postcolonial politics. A second problem lies in the implicit model of political culture it employs. The existence of 'factions' can be treated not as a product of particular political histories – histories of different communities' relations with the colonial and postcolonial state – but as a simple expression of some trans-historical essence, 'Indian' political culture.

The kind of approach to politics typified by the work on Indian factions in the 1960s suffered from two related lacunae. One is the absence of political ideology and the other is the absence of political solidarity. For example, in a paper from the late 1960s entitled 'Structures of Politics in the Villages of Southern Asia', Ralph Nicholas starts with the question 'What are the objectives of political activity in Indian villages?' Before proceeding to a comparative analysis of political divisions he discusses various definitional problems in the study of 'political activity'. For Nicholas 'political activity' is restricted to 'organized conflict over public power' and, as he is the first to admit, this eliminates any discussion of 'administration, government, or the direction of public policy in South Asian villages' (Nicholas 1968: 245). In other words the question of the broader goals of political activity – what you do when you attain power, or what you say you will do when you attain power, or how you respond to different politicians' assertions of what they will do when they attain power – this whole area, which we could call political ideology or political values, is left unconsidered. Factional analysis concerned itself with the vertical ties between leaders and followers. In describing these ties, the assumption tended to be that people mobilize politically in response to perceptions of their own self-interest. Hardiman, in his critical analysis of factional studies in the first volume of Subaltern Studies, points out numerous cases of caste or village solidarities in the literature on South Asian politics, horizontal solidarities which can be found behind alleged factional alignments. In particular he shows how little effect the control of patronage had on political action during the nationalist agitation in Gujerat in the 1920s and 1930s (Hardiman 1982). Although Hardiman's purpose is to advance the claims of class analysis over factional analysis in understanding South Asian politics, his evidence actually points in a different direction. The most spectacular examples of mass political mobilization in postcolonial South Asia have involved religious, linguistic, or regional identities – the phenomena known variously as communalism, nationalism, and fundamentalism – and few analysts would now claim that these can be straightforwardly reduced to class forces. Instead, as I shall argue later, we need to turn to the workings of representative democracy if we wish to get a better purchase on the ways in which an inchoate sense of 'us' and 'them', friend and enemy, may be hardened into the apparently implacable divisions of community found across contemporary South Asia.

Politics without the State

Whatever the reasons, political anthropology was in something of a rut by the mid-1970s and is only now beginning to re-emerge from that rut, albeit often under the strategic disguise of the 'anthropology of politics'. The dominant exploration of political themes in anthropology in the intervening years came in the form of the anthropology of power and resistance. In the late 1980s I took my tales of village politics and village nationalism on tour through some of the better-known and more theoretically advanced sites of North American anthropology. The results were not an overwhelming success. 'Where are the bodies?' I was asked; 'Where is the resistance?' My answers failed to impress.

The rise and fall of resistance studies still awaits its chronicler, and I will offer the most sketchy outline here. In anthropology, the theme announced itself in the near-simultaneous publication of a number of monographs in the mid-1980s (e.g. Comaroff 1985; Ong 1987). Perhaps the most influential of these was the work of a political-scientist-turned-ethnographer, James Scott's *Weapons of the Weak* (1985), which detailed the many small manifestations of 'everyday resistance' from the labourers in a Malaysian village undergoing a radical transformation of productive relations. Scott's work was explicitly intended to mark a break from the concern with overt rebellion which had emerged in the peasant studies of the Vietnam era, studies to which he had made his own notable contributions. The historians of the Subaltern Studies group, which began publishing collectively in the early 1980s, also started from a concern with tangible moments of rebellion which, they argued, had been edited out of the nationalist narratives of modern Indian history (Guha 1983), and moved toward the domestic and the everyday, while key members of its editorial collective drifted away from their initial Marxist positions and towards the mélange of structuralist and poststructuralist influences, literary critics now simply refer to as 'Theory'. Anthropological work on resistance rarely dwelt on the relationship between everyday micro-politics and the broader mobilizations that had been studied by historians of the peasantry from the 1960s on.[5] Their obvious debts were to the British cultural Marxists, E. P. Thompson and especially Raymond Williams, as filtered through the influence of the Birmingham Centre for Cultural Studies under the direction of Stuart Hall in the 1970s. Hall and his associates produced a loose synthesis of Marxist, structuralist and poststructuralist ideas around culture, power, and language, and a series of collective volumes combining theoretical pieces with (more or less) empirical analyses of popular culture in late 1970s Britain. By the early 1990s the anthropology of domination and resistance, hegemony and counter-hegemony, had become sufficiently institutionalized and ubiquitous to attract a scathing attack from Marshall Sahlins for its 'power functionalism' which reduced everything specific to a particular situation to the working through of a monolithic 'power', while simultaneously elevating the political import of the most trivial of everyday trivia (Sahlins 2002).

Although the work carried out within the broad paradigm of resistance studies had its own distinctive air of righteous struggle, it is worth remembering how much of its intellectual roots lie in moments of political defeat. British cultural Marxists like Raymond Williams and E. P. Thompson wrote their most influential work in the shadows cast by the Soviet invasion of Hungary, and later by the political disappointments of Wilson's 1960s Labour government. Their successors at the Birmingham Centre for Cultural Studies were intellectual refugees from the early years of Thatcherism. In India, the Subaltern Studies project was born out of the ashes of the early 1970s Naxalite agitations, and the bitter political

---

[5] The groundwork for the efflorescence of resistance studies from the mid-1980s onward can be found in early classics by Thompson (1963) and Williams (1958), refracted through the Gramscian and Althusserian enthusiasms of the late 1970s (Hall and Jefferson 1976; Williams 1977; Willis 1977). As well as the important works cited here, useful points of entry to the anthropological literature in this tradition (not least because of their critical take on some of the key terms of debate) include Abu-Lughod (1990), Lave et al. (1992), Ortner (1995), and Crehan (2002).

disillusion of Indira Gandhi's Emergency. In all these cases, the pursuit of politics and political struggle in other places not normally thought of as political – in domesticity, styles of dress, religious, and other idioms – was a kind of redemptive act, a gesture of hope in an otherwise bleak political landscape. The price, though, could be either indifference, or even hostility, to what people themselves might take to be the political.

A good empirical example of this can be found in Scott's own ethnography (1985). Scott's *Weapons of the Weak* is a meticulous account of the ways in which agricultural labourers in a village in Malaysia undermine the authority and power of the local landowners. Sherry Ortner (1995: 181) has pointed out how an emphasis on political-economic dimensions of resistance in this study results in relative ethnographic deafness to the important nexus of religion and power in Scott's field locale. But as well as sabotaging the farm machinery, passing on apocalyptic rumours, and swapping counter-hegemonic gossip about their local oppressors, people in Sedaka also do quite a bit of politics. Scott is too scrupulous an ethnographer not to record this, but the facts of local politics are left outside his dominant narrative, and dealt with in a voice of mild puzzlement. Party political alignments do not entirely make sense in class terms. Why do a minority of villagers, some rich but mostly poor, align themselves with the opposition party when there is no possible material advantage in so doing? Why invest passion in such an apparently pointless identification? In running through the reasons for such an apparently pointless investment in political identification, Scott ends up with the half-hearted categories 'moral appeal' and 'sheer pride and stubbornness' (Scott 1985: 134–5).

The literature on resistance is too large and diverse to allow of easy generalizations. Instead I want to pick up one particular strand of that work, that found in the early volumes of Subaltern Studies, and examine in more detail its idea of what may count as political in India. There are two reasons for this particular choice of example. One is that the Subaltern project, while undeniably various in its individual manifestations, nevertheless has in the programmatic writings of Ranajit Guha provided one of the most theoretically coherent accounts of its analytic practice. The other is that a great deal of the work published in the Subaltern Studies series has focused on my central concern, broadly speaking the relationship between culture and the colonial (and sometimes postcolonial) state.

Like the work of the Birmingham school, the Subaltern Studies project was, according to its founding editor, conceived in a moment of political disillusion. While the 1970s in Britain now feel like the preparation for the long years of Thatcherism, the same decade in India started with the abortive agrarian risings of the Naxalites, followed by Mrs Gandhi's invocation of Emergency rule, and finally the collapse of the anti-Indira opposition coalition. That disillusion provoked two questions for the founders:

1. What was there in our colonial past and our engagement with nationalism to land us in our current predicament – that is the aggravating and seemingly insoluble difficulties of the nation-state?
2. How are the unbearable difficulties of our current condition compatible with and explained by what happened during colonial rule and our predecessors' engagement with the politics and culture of that period? (Guha 1997: xi)

I shall return to the best-known Subaltern argument on the nation-state, that found in Partha Chatterjee's *Nationalist Thought and the Colonial World* (Chatterjee 1986), in the next chapter. Here I want to concentrate on the issue of politics and culture, and specifically the place of the state.

Radical historical work on the central themes of the Subaltern project – on peasants and peasant consciousness, and history from below – had been appearing since the late 1950s, and had gained pace with the Vietnam War and the consequent interest in the radical potential of Third World peasant societies: James Scott's early book on the *Moral Economy of the Peasant* (Scott 1976), which transposed an idea from E. P. Thompson to Southeast Asian peasant insurrections, would be a case in point. But the Subaltern project added three important ingredients. One was the attention to colonialism as the governing frame for their work, and especially the enduring effects of colonial rule in the politics of the present: here their work chimed perfectly with what was to become the postcolonial wave in the humanities and the social sciences. The second was the sheer polemical force of some of their publications, especially of Guha's editorial contribution. The third was the theoretical space they marked out for themselves, between the Gramscian Marxism of the early volumes, from whence the allusion to the 'subaltern' itself came, and the increasing turn towards poststructural literary theory in later volumes: again this was precisely the space about to be explored by the cultural left, especially in North America. In defining, 'subaltern' as 'a name for the general attribute of subordination in South Asian society whether this is expressed in terms of class, caste, age, gender and office or in any other way' (Guha 1982b: vii), Guha also signalled a move away from more conventional class politics and towards the emerging politics of identity.

Guha sets out his theoretical stall in the first volume of Subaltern Studies, in a short piece entitled 'On Some Aspects of the Historiography of Colonial India' (Guha 1982a). The problem with previous historical writing on colonial India, he starts, is its bias toward the colonial and indigenous elites. What this history cannot acknowledge is the autonomous role of popular action, especially in the course of the nationalist movement:

This inadequacy of elitist historiography follows directly from the narrow and partial view of politics to which it is committed by virtue of its class outlook. In all writings of this kind the parameters of Indian politics are assumed to be or enunciated as exclusively or primarily those of the institutions introduced by the British for the government of the country and the corresponding sets of laws, policies, attitudes and other elements of the superstructure. (Guha 1982a: 3–4)

In contrast to this narrow identification of politics with the workings of the colonial state, Guha identifies what he calls 'the politics of the people' (Guha 1982a: 4):

This was an *autonomous* domain, for it neither originated from elite politics nor did its existence depend on the latter. It was traditional only in so far as its roots could be traced back to pre-colonial times but it was by no means archaic in the sense of being outmoded. Far from being destroyed or rendered virtually ineffective, as was elite politics of the traditional type by the intrusion of colonialism, it continued to operate vigorously in spite of the latter, adjusting itself to the conditions prevailing under the Raj and in many respects developing entirely new strains in both form and content. (Guha 1982a: 4)

Such popular political forms can be seen in the history of the nationalist movement.

A brilliant example of the terrain that Guha has identified can be seen in Shahid Amin's essay on 'Gandhi as Mahatma', published in the third volume of Subaltern Studies (Amin 1984). This uses local press reports from the early 1920s to reconstruct something of the peasant perception of Gandhi at that time. Clearly, many peasants responded to Gandhi in what might be loosely characterized as a 'religious' idiom: seeking *darshan* (the gift of sight or appearance, usually received from an image of a god or from a holy man), expressing their *bhakti* or devotion, arriving in huge crowds to greet his train as it arrives in a district. But the local press also report various supernatural manifestations and rumours which attribute magical powers to Gandhi. (My favourite is the headline 'Gandhi in dream: Englishmen run away naked' (Amin 1984: 25).) Amin collects and collates these tales in order to make his main point – that understandings and expectations of Gandhi as seen, as it were, from below, were often very different from the official Congress version. Moreover, there was little if anything Congress leaders could do to control the spread of rumours and legends about the Mahatma. Here is an example of the autonomous domain of people's politics, to borrow Guha's terms: as much 'religious' as 'political' in its idioms, generating horizontal solidarities, and apparently quite separate from the actions, let alone the control, of elite politicians.

Guha's most elaborate account of his ideas of the place of politics in colonial India can be found in the long essay 'Dominance without hegemony and its historiography', published in *Subaltern Studies VI* (Guha 1989). Here he elaborates on what he described in the earlier paper as the 'structural dichotomy' between elite and popular politics (Guha 1982a: 6). The central point of the later essay is captured in its title: the colonial state exercised 'dominance', primarily through coercion, but not 'hegemony'. In other words, the coercive apparatus of the colonial state penetrated Indian society very deeply indeed, but the ideological apparatus failed to reach much below the higher levels of the Indian elite. At the heart of Guha's argument is a model of domination and subordination, persuasion and coercion, collaboration and resistance. On to this model Guha maps two radically different politicial idioms, one British and based in liberal theory, the other Indian, often religious in its vocabulary, and elucidated by Guha with reference to classic Orientalist sources like the Laws of Manu and the Bhagavad-Gita: order vs *danda*, improvement vs *dharma*, obedience vs *bhakti*, and what he calls 'rightful dissent' vs 'dharmic protest'.

The relation between the two idioms, or paradigms as he sometimes refers to them, is not a simple one:

The ordering of these idioms for discursive purposes is of course not quite the same thing as it is in the actual practice of politics. In the latter, each particular instance acquires its specificity from the braiding, collapsing, echoing and blending of these idioms in such a way as to baffle all description of this process merely as an interaction between a dynamic modernity and an inert tradition, or as the mechanical stapling of a classic Western liberalism to an unchanging Eastern feudal culture. (Guha 1989: 270)

The next chapter of this book is about just this process of 'braiding, collapsing, echoing and blending', so we will return to Guha's metaphors of interaction there. To give this rather austere model some flesh and blood, we need simply return to the examples with which I opened this chapter. Burghart's account of politics, protest, and agency within a 'lordly culture' self-consciously reconstructs an indigenous political idiom, very like the one Guha describes. Adams' disaffected post-democrats may be read as braiding the languages, and moral assumptions, of two very different political idioms as best they can. Similarly Alter's wrestlers apparently evaluate an object from one idiom, the post-Independence state, in the language of the other, dharmic order.

But Guha takes the argument a stage further. In order to cement his central claim about dominance without hegemony, and to substantiate his ancillary claim that the colonial state represents the limit of the universalizing force of capital, he needs to make one more claim about the colonial state. Why, he asks, did the colonial state co-exist with this radically different political culture? The answer lies in the nature of the colonial state. This did not 'originate from' local society: 'No moment of that society's internal dynamics was involved in the imposition of the alien authority structure'. The state, therefore, exists as 'an *absolute externality . . structured like a despotism*, with no mediating depths, no space provided for a transaction between the will of the rulers and that of the ruled' (Guha 1989: 274). In other words, Guha is insisting on a radical break between state and society, with the state only ever imaginable as something emanating from outside the local social order. And, lest we think this only refers to the colonial state, he closes the essay with an allusion to 'the character of the successor regime too as a dominance without hegemony' (Guha 1989: 307).

Here then, we may find, in an unusually clear and theorized form, an explanation for the most obvious lacuna in the literature of resistance: the world of organized politics, with its elections, spectacles, feats of outlandish representation, outbreaks of violence, and endless capacity for moral alarm. All of this is, as it were, outside the frame. In the literature on resistance, the state is never a resource, or a place to seek justice, let

alone a zone of hope, however distant or deferred, in the political imaginary. It is, if it appears at all, an 'absolute externality', a source of coercion,
violence, or fear; and thus the only theoretically correct response to the
state is resistance. I am, of course, extemporizing into territory not cov-
ered in Guha's article, but a sense of the state as 'absolute externality' is
precisely what we find, again and again, in the anthropological literature
on resistance. It is not, however, quite what we find ethnographically,
as I shall show in chapter six. Writing of the influence of the Subaltern project on Indian agrarian history, David Ludden complains that
it 'constituted agrarian realities that lacked political parties, economic
development, class structures, technological change, and social mobil-
ity' (Ludden 2001: 208). I would argue that many of the anthropologists
trained in the shadow of the Subaltern project (mostly, that is, in the
rather un-Subaltern halls of the big US research universities) have been
unable to acknowledge the centrality of these issues to the people whose
lives and aspirations they want to record. Like the historians criticized by
Ludden, they too have implicitly endorsed the vision of the rural subaltern as inhabiting a quite other world to the urban elite. This is especially
unfortunate because the decades in which the Subaltern project rose to
intellectual eminence outside India saw unprecedented levels of political
engagement among the poorest and most dispossessed strata in Indian
society (Corbridge and Harriss 2000). This so-called 'democratization of
Indian democracy' is one of the crucial backdrops for my argument in
this book.

Which is not to diminish in any way the achievements of Guha and
his colleagues. The political world of non-elite Indians which they have
attempted to recover and interpret is a much richer and more interesting object than the increasingly eviscerated politics of the 1960s political
anthropologists. As an intellectual project, Subaltern Studies was conceived in conscious opposition to work in Indian history which, in some
respects paralleled that kind of political anthropology. Guha explicitly
presents his programme as a critique of the type of history associated

with Anil Seal and his colleagues in the so-called 'Cambridge School'. That history, which focused on the administrative structures of the colonial state, and the co-option of local elites into those structures, might be seen in retrospect as analogous to the more positivistic, and a-cultural, tendency in political anthropology. It also, though, blurred the boundary between colonizer and colonized, elite collaborator and nationalist resister, and one of Guha's aims is to restore those boundaries, by insisting on a world of Indian politics, conducted in Indian idioms, which survived the transition to colonialism more or less intact. Its appeal to anthropologists of a romantic but oppositional disposition should be obvious. Even as the discipline's internal critics pointed to the political dangers of its visions of separate cultural worlds and timeless primitivism (e.g. Fabian 1983), here was an apparently radical critique which allowed for the reinvention of the classic anthropological object, only this time revalued as a source of resistance and struggle. This issue of the boundaries between local cultural resources and apparently external institutional structures is the subject of the next chapter.

THREE

Culture, Nation, and Misery

Culture and Conversation

We need to press the issue of translation a little harder. In this book I
want to combine some of the themes that remained resolutely separated
in the discussion in the last chapter. I want to show how the political
has come to be constituted in different parts of the postcolonial world,
as something unimaginable in its current form without the institutional
framework of the postcolonial state, but also as something whose story
cannot be simply contained within the known history of that institutional
framework. In this chapter I will do this by returning to the paradoxes
raised by the cultural interpretation of new, 'modern', institutions and
practices, suggesting that these institutions and practices never simply
carry their own stories immanent within them, but in fact are understood in whatever idiom comes to hand. Political modernity is a diverse
modernity, because different people bring different histories, values, and
expectations to their encounters with its apparently invariant forms. But
the political itself is not a static object mutely awaiting its local interpretation. It is a field of tremendous potential productivity and danger,
never less than disturbing, and often seemingly capable of blowing away
received expectations in very different areas of life. I will start to elaborate
on this sense of the political in the next chapter, but here I want to stay
with the issue of the translation of political forms into new settings.

The political form whose translation has been the focus of most attention in recent years is that thing that we call 'nationalism'. Nationalism is especially interesting from this point of view because it seems to embody some of the central paradoxes in this whole area of enquiry. It is a political force which argues for the uniqueness of each of its own manifestations, but everywhere does so in an apparently similar way. It often invokes a deep past, but such invocations turn out on inspection to be quite new. It especially disturbs anthropologists because, as I explained in chapter one to this book, it seems to mock their very project: making cultural difference into the stuff of intolerance and hatred. Anti-colonial movements across the colonized world struggled against colonialism and European domination in pursuit of the same *telos*, the apparently 'Western' political model of the nation-state. In his *Imagined Communities* (cf. Anderson 1983), Benedict Anderson described this in terms of a modular diffusion of the ideal of the nation-state from European and Latin American origins out across the non-Western world. The implications of this version of anti-colonial nationalism are the subject of Partha Chatterjee's *Nationalist Thought and the Colonial World* (Chatterjee 1986), and that book will provide the focus for a later section in this chapter. The final part of the chapter returns briefly to Sri Lanka, and the recent nationalist critique of 'Western' anthropology there – a critique which restores anthropology itself to the space of the political.

Let me start, though, with the idea of conversation. What new kinds of conversations were made possible in the colonial context and what kinds have become increasingly difficult if not impossible? One answer can be found in a wonderfully poignant scene in Amitav Ghosh's historical-autobiographical-ethnographic novel-travelogue *In an Antique Land* (Ghosh 1992). Ghosh himself was born in India, received an Oxford D.Phil. in the early 1980s for his anthropological study of an Egyptian village, and has since published a number of well-received novels. He now lives in New York. The book cuts between two time-frames and two apparently very different themes. There is a vivid account of Ghosh's anthropological fieldwork in Egypt in the early 1980s and there is Ghosh's historical reconstruction of the life of a twelfth-century Indian slave, based on documents from a collection of medieval Jewish manuscripts found at the end of the last century in the synagogue of the Palestinians in Fustat in Cairo (Ghosh 1993). *In an Antique Land*, like all of Ghosh's earlier work, is informed by a particular vision of the once vibrant network of traders and scholars, who moved between India and what is now the Middle East and North Africa: for Ghosh the vision above all means a world before nation-states, political boundaries and the consciously erected walls modern people place around their communities of faith and language.

In this scene, Ghosh, the young Indian in rural Egypt, is having to explain and defend Indian barbarism, this time to a sceptical Imam. After an opening exchange on cow worship, the Imam announces to their audience that 'they', Indians like the young anthropologist, burn their dead. Ghosh counters by pointing out that even Europeans are known to burn their dead. The Imam is scornful: 'They don't burn their dead in the West. They're not an ignorant people. They're advanced, they're educated, they have science, they have guns and tanks and bombs.' Unwillingly Ghosh finds himself drawn into an increasingly absurd argument: 'we' Indians, he blurts out, have guns and bombs too, better than Egypt's, we've even had a nuclear explosion. Ghosh records his immediate shame and dismay at his own outburst: 'the Imam and I had participated in our final defeat, in the dissolution of centuries of dialogue that had linked us: we had demonstrated the irreversible triumph of the language that had usurped all the others in which people once discussed their differences' (Ghosh 1992: 236). For Ghosh, the 'language that had usurped all the others' is the language of science, development, the nation-state, and the modern political community. What comes after colonialism is a closing down of conversation and dialogue, even between people from places which had been linked by trade and religion and (though Ghosh makes less of this) war and conquest, long before the relatively brief period of European rule. The Indian and the Imam find themselves forced to trade words in the brutal *lingua franca* of modern geo-politics: our guns are bigger than your guns.

Ghosh's reading of this scene is unusually eloquent and moving, but in other respects it is in keeping with a whole body of recent argument about the failure of postcolonial politics, a body of argument or, to use the term I will employ later, a 'structure of feeling' summed up in Partha Chatterjee's allusion to 'our post-colonial misery'. Chatterjee's diagnosis concentrates on 'our surrender to the old forms of the modern state' (Chatterjee 1993: 11), a formulation which echoes Guha's talk of 'our current predicament – that is the aggravating and seemingly insoluble difficulties of the nation-state' (Guha 1997: xi).

It is salutary, though, to contrast this interpretation of the modern as somehow restricting the possibilities of dialogue, with the more optimistic views of radical intellectuals at the end of the period of formal colonial rule. A few years after the scene at my leave-taking ceremony described in chapter one, I was trying to write a paper which would help me sort out the implications, for an anthropology of nationalism, of the fact that Sri Lankan nationalists of whatever persuasion employed concepts of 'culture' which were demonstrably similar to the anthropological usages I had been trained to regard as my own disciplinary property. What I found and what I did with it is mostly another story, which I have told elsewhere (Spencer 1990c), except for one thing. In a neglected corner of the library I found a collection of essays from the early 1950s by the journalist and novelist Martin Wickramasinghe (1891–1976), a central figure in the history of twentieth-century Sinhala writing. In the essays I was surprised to find not merely a lot of use of ideas from mid-century anthropology (from Hocart, Herskovits, Benedict, and above all Malinowski) but also what struck me as an engagingly subtle approach to the understanding of issues of cultural borrowing and authenticity:

Our borrowing or even wholesale adaptation of European cultural elements will not produce that particular culture here. Borrowing and adaptation produce only a new culture. It is neither the old culture nor the borrowed culture. It is a new culture or a complex or an institution born as a result of new contacts. When alien cultural elements come in contact they produce changes in each other. By fusion of these changed elements, new customs or institutions are produced, and they become functional and integral parts of the original culture which came in contact with the new. (Wickramasinghe 1973 [1952]: 124)

I want to pause briefly with this vision of cultural difference in order to effect a contrast with recent writing on culture, colonialism, and political modernity. In particular I want to reconstruct two contexts for Wickramasinghe's argument.

The first is the Sri Lankan context of the time, when Wickramasinghe was arguing against two rather different groups: what he saw as the rootless English-speaking elite, but also the more inward-looking elements of the nationalist movement. Where some of his contemporaries were busy trying to reconstruct a Sinhala past purged of all external – in this case, Indian – influences, Wickramasinghe happily acknowledged the importance of 'cultural elements' 'borrowed from India' (Wickramasinghe 1973 [1952]: 8). And he was quick to defend the vitality of village folk culture in the face of what he saw as the insecure snobbery of the anglophone elite. His own position was that Sinhalese culture was indeed 'ancient', but it was not unchanging; indeed one of its most enduring characteristics was precisely what he called its 'elasticity' (Wickramasinghe 1973 [1952]: 121). I don't want to exaggerate the subtlety or originality of Wickramasinghe's argument. The same tension between radical historicism (a culture is merely an assemblage of components from elsewhere) and romantic culturalism (but each culture puts those components together according to its own particular *geist* or genius) is one animating force in the work of the great German-American anthropologist Franz Boas (e.g., Boas 1982[1898]).[1] Nevertheless, an essentialism in which what is essential is the capacity to adapt to new circumstances is, intellectually and politically, a considerable improvement on most rival accounts of cultural continuity. It also allows Wickramasinghe to uphold a pluralist version of political modernity: 'Only unprogressive nations, to hide the sterility of their souls, seek indigenous or supernatural origins for their institutions and culture. Progressive nations borrow cultural elements from everywhere and assert their virile genius in remoulding and recreating them' (Wickramasinghe 1973 [1952]: 11).

Wickramasinghe is here following closely one part of the argument in Malinowski's posthumous *Dynamics of Culture Change* (Malinowski 1945). Few readers bother much with Malinowski's later writing on colonialism and change these days, yet they contain a number of surprises. On the one hand they seem to reveal in an especially frank form all sorts of interesting internal contradictions in the relationship between 1930s British anthropology and its colonial paymasters. But they also reveal equally interesting contradictions in Malinowski's attitude to what was then conventionally described as 'culture contact', a phrase which in practice almost always meant colonial rule. From the early 1930s onward, Malinowski argued strongly against what he saw as anthropology's antiquarian tendency to filter out all signs of the modern in ethnographic accounts of other societies, in favour of the construction or reconstruction of some version of the traditional and unchanging. Malinowski's anthropology was based on three principles: radical empiricism (his espousal of deep fieldwork), radical holism (his somewhat ramshackle functionalism), and radical presentism (his opposition to evolutionist

---

[1] Many of the same issues recur, for example, in Lévi-Strauss's great volumes on mythology, in which cultural elements – in this case myths – are tracked from one setting to another, and the work of each culture's *geist* is found in the way that structures are transformed and retransformed in their passage from group to group. More generally, see Sahlins (Sahlins 1999) for a persuasive reminder that anti-essentialism in anthropological accounts of culture wasn't born yesterday.

reconstruction). So the study of changing societies should concentrate on the whole society, as encountered by the ethnographer in the present, and without any special account of the different historical origins of the various practices and institutions thus observed. The argument hinges on the moment that Malinowski calls 'transculturation':

The phenomena of culture change are entirely new cultural realities which have to be studied in their own right . . . Even when we know all the 'ingredients' which go to make up a mine or a school, we cannot foretell or foresee what the development of such a new institution will be. For the forces brought into being and determining the course of growth and development are not 'borrowed' but have been born within the new institution. (Malinowski 1938: xxiv)

The last point is crucial; when institutions are transplanted into different settings we cannot assume that they carry within them an inevitable teleology, a script that will be worked out regardless of local circumstances. Rather each may develop in new and unpredictable ways.[2]

It is these arguments of Malinowski's which are quoted most enthusiastically by Wickramasinghe, himself writing in quite different circumstances and with somewhat different concerns from Malinowski. They link him to a third figure in my late colonial intellectual triangulation, the Cuban writer Fernando Ortiz who coined the term 'transculturation'

[2] Malinowski's theories of culture change were famously attacked by Gluckman soon after his death (Gluckman 1949), in terms that continue to reverberate in more recent scholarship on colonialism and postcolonialism, especially in Africa (Ferguson 1999: 26). One of Gluckman's central points was that, for all the local variations one might reasonably expect, a great deal of what we need to know about labour relations in an African mine is broadly similar to what we know about labour relations in other capitalist institutions in other times and places (Gluckman 1949: 12–3). A concentration on cultural novelty renders comparison, of the sociological kind favoured by Gluckman, impossible. But also, lurking in the background of Gluckman's fierce critique, there lies his concern for the political implications, in a South Africa entering the years of official Apartheid, of all claims to cultural difference. James, and more recently, Stocking, between them give a good sense of the complexity of Malinowski's response to colonialism (James 1973; Stocking 1983; Stocking 1991).

and employed it in his book *Cuban Counterpoint* in 1940. Ortiz was a writer, a cultural polymath, an ethnographer, and above all ethnomusicologist, founder of the Institute of Afro-Cuban studies in Cuba, and sometime associate of Malinowski (who contributed an introduction to the first edition of *Cuban Counterpoint*). Ortiz was struggling to understand Cuba, and especially to find room for the different cultural and social components – African, European, American – which had been brought together in contemporary Cuba. His neologism 'transculturation' served two purposes: it avoided the implicit asymmetry in the more common term 'acculturation', which suggested that the 'problem' was the more or less gradual acquisition of one culture (usually that of the colonizer) by a member of another culture (usually one of the colonized); and it carried within it a sense of process and incompleteness:

There was no more important factor in the evolution of Cuba than these continuous, radical, contrasting geographic transmigrations, economic and social, of the first settlers, this perennial transitory nature of their objectives... Men, economies, cultures, ambitions were all foreigners here, provisional, changing, 'birds of passage' over the country, at its cost, against its wishes, and without its approval. (Ortiz 1995 [1947]: 101; cf. Pérez Firmat 1989: 23)[3]

What links these three figures, I would suggest, is a particular late colonial structure of feeling. They are all looking for ways to come to terms with the complex social and cultural impact of colonialism, without reducing it to a unidirectional process of 'Westernization', or as the term would be used in the years that followed, 'modernization'. The impact of the modern could not be ignored or wished away, but it was possible to understand it as potentially plural, as giving birth to many different forms as it found its way into many different settings. Clearly there are problems with their formulation: as with the term 'creolization', which has had a recent vogue in anthropology, there is a strong implication that any fluid,

---

[3] For more recent commentary on Ortiz see Davies and Fardon (1991), Davies (2000), and Coronil (1995[1947]).

modern situation is the product of the interaction of two otherwise dis-crete and fixed parent cultures (Hannerz 1987). And there are differences amongst these three in the inflections the idea of transculturation takes: Wickramasinghe's ringing endorsement of the 'virile genius' of 'progres-sive nations' stands in contrast to Ortiz's more poignant account of the comprehensive suffering that accompanied the making of modern Cuba, while Malinowski, not uncharacteristically, tries to have it both ways. Both Ortiz and Wickramasinghe argued unsuccessfully for the establishment of cultural anthropology as a central discipline in their countries, while Malinowski, as was his habit, used his introduction to Ortiz's book to set out a plea for sponsorship of Latin American studies by the 'great and richly endowed cultural foundations of the United States' (Malinowski 1995 [1947]: xvi).

In short, we have here a moment when it seemed to be not just possible but necessary to rethink the idea of culture as essentially bounded, and to turn instead to a much more open vision of the permeability of what were conventionally seen as closed cultural islands. That open vision has much in common with Ghosh's vision of a world of movements and accommodations and dialogues. But in the half-century between Ghosh and these three late colonial intellectuals something tragic has clearly hap-pened, for the political circumstances which had once seemed to open up the possibility for new accommodations and dialogues, however painful, are now seen to have silenced them for ever: 'to make ourselves under-stood, we had both resorted, I, a student of the "humane" sciences, and he, an old-fashioned village Imam, to the very terms that world leaders and statesmen use at great, global conferences, the universal, irresistible metaphysic of modern meaning' (Ghosh 1992: 237).

Malinowski's Ambivalence

I shall return to Ghosh's allegedly universal and irresistible metaphysic in due course. First, though, I want to explore the implications of my

Cuban–Polish–Sinhalese triangulation a little bit further, not least because I believe that ideas like Ortiz's transculturation, if pushed far enough, can start to dissolve the sense of irresistibility and universality which Ghosh laments. The issue has been of some importance to *fin-de-siècle* anthropologists, because if the political language of modernity, however singular in appearance, turns out to be plural in interpretation; if there are what Charles Taylor (Taylor 1995) has termed 'alternative modernities' concealed behind the familiar façade of the nation-state, then political anthropology has a new, and potentially exciting, task in front of it.

I shall start with Malinowski. By his own account, the moment of transculturation came in the context of a meeting with Ortiz in Havana in 1939 (Malinowski 1995 [1947]: lvii), although the grounds for his enthusiastic adoption of the idea had been prepared throughout his writings of the 1930s on issues of 'culture contact' and change.[4] Starting from his lobbying of the Rockefeller Foundation for support for his programme of 'Practical Anthropology' at the International African Institute in 1929, Malinowski's pronouncements on colonial rule were, in George Stocking's words 'spoken in different voices to different audiences'. So, for example, in South Africa in 1933, Malinowski told a White audience that Africans needed education of a sort which would not 'develop in him claims and desires which his future salary and status will never satisfy', while telling a Black audience that anthropology's task was to 'recognize the detribalized African and fight for his place in the world'. And, Stocking drily notes, having received an enthusiastic reception for this argument, 'Malinowski filed the talk away in a folder with the annotation "Nig Lec."' (Stocking 1991: 56). In 1936 he appealed for Lord Lugard's support in a bid to raise funds for Kenyatta's research by stressing the ways in which Kenyatta's earlier 'political bias' had been 'almost completely

---

[4] Davies (2000) dates the meeting with Malinowski as 1937. The Venezuelan anthropologist Fernando Coronil, in his Introduction to the 1995 edition of *Cuban Counterpoint*, provides a useful commentary on Malinowski's use of the idea of transculturation (Coronil 1995).

eradicated' by the influence of anthropology and its scientific method, but two years later commended Kenyatta in print for penetrating beyond the 'pretences' of the Dual Mandate (Stocking 1991: 57). Most strikingly of all, in his 1938 Introductory Essay to the International African Institute collection *Methods of Study of Culture Contact in Africa* he lampoons the idea that Europeans simply 'give' the fruits of their civilization to their colonial subjects:

In fact from all points here enumerated, it would be easy to see that it is not a matter of 'give', nor yet a matter of generous 'offering', but usually a matter of 'take'. Lands have been alienated from Africans to a large extent, and usually in the most fruitful regions. Tribal sovereignty and the indulgence in warfare, which the African valued even as we seem to value it, has been taken away from him. He is being taxed, but the disposal of the funds thus provided is not always under his control, and never completely so. The labour which he has to give is voluntary only in name. (Malinowski 1938: xxiii)

Then, just as Malinowski's polemic reaches its peak, we are blandly assured that 'This is not an indictment nor a piece of pro-native pleading' (Malinowski 1938: xxiv).

The context for this equivocation is straightforwardly political, and Malinowski's ambivalent pronouncements on emerging African nationalism can be interpreted fairly simply in terms of the pull of his own political sympathies – 'I for one believe in the anthropologist's being not only the interpreter of the native but also his champion' (Stocking 1991: 57) – versus the need to convince the powers-that-be of anthropology's practical usefulness to the colonial project. Even so, comparable inconsistencies lurk at the heart of his intellectual response to colonial societies. We might start at the end, with Malinowski's confession of omissions in his final Trobriand work, *Coral Gardens and their Magic*. Here Malinowski referred to his earlier pursuit of the 'real savage' (in preference to the 'changing Melanesian' he found himself actually observing) as the 'most serious shortcoming' of all his Melanesian research and he attributed this error to his lingering attachment to the 'antiquarian' anthropology of his youth (Malinowski 1935: 479–81). In his 1938 IAI Introduction, Malinowski expanded upon this empiricist insistence on the study of the here and now, on the need to see the present as it is and to ignore the temptation to construct a more 'anthropologically correct' account of a situation by filtering out the contaminating presence of the colonial world. Commenting on the work of the different contributors to the collection – which included Richards, Fortes, Schapera, and Mair – Malinowski challenges certain key arguments. He protests at the assumption, which he detects in the essays by Fortes and Schapera, that it is possible to study a colonial situation as a stable, functioning whole: 'change' and some 'maladjustment' are inevitable. He then challenges Monica Hunter's assertion that understanding of change first requires the disentangling of indigenous from external cultural elements: 'The task of the field-worker cannot consist in disengaging and re-assorting the black and white elements of the cultural conglomerate, for the reality of culture change is not a conglomerate, nor a mixture, nor yet a juxtaposition of partially fused elements' (Malinowski 1938: xxi). (This incoherent set of negatives is surprisingly close to Guha's 'braiding, collapsing, echoing and blending' discussed in the last chapter.) And against Schapera, Malinowski criticizes the alleged need to reconstruct what he calls the 'zero-point' of change, the state of affairs before the encounter with the colonial power. What is of interest to the fieldworker is the remembered past, with its powerful psychological weight in the present, which is not at all the same thing as the past as it actually was (Malinowski 1938: xxv–xxixii).

Already one inconsistency begins to emerge in the argument. On the one hand, the kind of situation Malinowski is commenting on is not at all stable: change is of the essence. On the other hand, the fieldworker must always proceed on the basis of her observations in the present and try to avoid the confusions consequent upon a comparison between the empirical present and the reconstructed past. How then can the fieldworker apprehend the reality of change without some attempt to trace the effects of time? The answer to this question is especially disappointing: 'The study of culture change must take into account three orders of reality: the impact of the higher culture; the substance of native life on which it is directed; and the phenomenon of autonomous change resulting from the reaction between the two cultures' (Malinowski 1938: xxiv). In other words, although the situation of change should not be seen as a 'conglomerate' or 'mixture' of separable elements, the analysis of change requires just such a separation of European from native from new. The banality of this approach is evident in Malinowski's posthumous *Dynamics of Culture Change*, where all the forbidden divisions ('surviving forms of tradition', 'reconstructed past') reappear as headings for specimen synoptic charts for the analysis of situations of change. And on these charts the most potentially interesting column ('new forces of spontaneous African reintegration or reaction') is embarrassingly empty (Malinowski 1945: 88–9; Coronil 1995[1947]: xxiii–xxiv).

We might be content to let matters rest there, but for one thing. The anglophone rediscovery of Ortiz's remarkable work connects with important recent arguments about the relationship between cultural difference and modernity, allowing us to re-evaluate the road not taken, for whatever reason, by Malinowski himself in his work on colonial change. In their contributions to *Cuban Counterpoint* each makes clear exactly what he finds appealing in the work of the other. For Malinowski, Ortiz's term 'transculturation' is greatly to be preferred to the then voguish term, 'acculturation':

Aside from the unpleasant way in which it falls upon the ear (it sounds like a cross between a hiccup and a belch), the word *acculturation* contains a number of definite and undesirable etymological implications. It is an ethnocentric word with a moral connotation. The immigrant has to *acculturate* himself; so do the natives, pagan or heathen, barbarian or savage, who enjoy being under the sway of our great Western culture . . . The 'uncultured' is to receive the benefit of 'our culture'; it is he who must change and become converted into 'one of us'. (Malinowski 1995 [1947]: lviii)

'Transculturation', in contrast, 'does not contain the implication of one certain culture toward which the other must tend, but an exchange between two cultures, both of them active, both contributing their share, and both co-operating to bring about a new reality of civilization' (Malinowski 1995 [1947]: lix). And Ortiz, in defending his neologism, invokes Malinowski's arguments on change:

> I am of the opinion that the word *transculturation* better expresses the different phases of the process of transition from one culture to another because this does not consist merely in acquiring another culture, which is what the English word *acculturation* really implies, but the process also necessarily involves the loss or uprooting of a previous culture, which could be defined as deculturation. In addition it carries the idea of the consequent creation of new cultural phenomena, which could be called neoculturation. In the end, as the school of Malinowski's followers maintains, the result of every union of cultures is similar to that of the reproductive process between individuals: the offspring always has something of both parents but is always different from each of them. (Ortiz 1995 [1947]: 102–3)

If we turn to the substance of Ortiz's study, we discover a much more intellectually promising model than that provided by Malinowski's dismal charts and columns. One obvious difference is Ortiz's use of history, something disingenuously acknowledged by Malinowski who attempts to use this as evidence of Ortiz's membership of his own exclusive order of functionalists (Malinowski 1995 [1947]: lxii). The first part of the book is the essay 'Cuban counterpoint' itself, which takes the form of an imagined conversation between the two great protagonists of Cuban history, tobacco and sugar, the native product and the colonial import. The attributes of the two are repeatedly contrasted, while their social and cultural implications are teased out and inspected at length. The form of the essay is truly remarkable because it suggests a way to resolve some of the tensions in Malinowski's essays on change. The contrapuntal movement between the stories of the two products allows Ortiz to *acknowledge* their different origins, but without *reducing* them to their origins: tobacco was found in Cuba, sugar was brought to Cuba, both facts are important, but what is equally important is what has happened to them, and to Cuba, since. Moving between the two, detailing their modes of production, their position in the global market, their homogeneity and their heterogeneity, Ortiz manages to convey a sense of change, of constant movement, and of potential movement to come. As one recent critic puts it:

His interpretation is far from mechanistic; he consistently deconstructs binary or Manichaean conceptualizations of colonial cultures. His writing – lyrical, suspenseful, witty, chaotic, exciting – captures all the dizzy turbulence, violence, panic, teror, pain, hopes, struggle and disillusions of this complex, overlapping series of cultural 'encounters'. Reading the compressed evocation of the dramatic process of Cuban cultural life gives the impression of whizzing through a tunnel in a time machine. (Davies 2000: 151)

And what he produces from all this is something still very rare: a kind of colonial history which is intelligible, indeed which extends intelligibility well beyond the modest boundaries of its immediate concerns, but which is manifestly not teleological.

This is as much a matter of form (dialogical, contrapuntal) and voice, as it is a question of substance. From the point of view of the writer, what is at stake in this move is not so much the now familiar project of delineating so-called 'alternative modernities', but rather the more specific possibility of creating, in writing and other forms of cultural production, an alternative *modernism*. This is not so much claiming that the modern world is inherently different in different settings; it is the hope that men and women retain the interpretive capacity to treat it differently. Marshall Berman opens his wonderful survey of modernism, *All that Is Solid Melts into Air* with a working definition of modernism as 'a struggle to make ourselves at home in a constantly changing world', providing 'an amazing variety of visions and ideas that aim to make men and women the subjects as well as the objects of modernization' (Berman 1988: 6, 16). So a writer like Wickramasinghe could at once be concerned to work with the distinctive resources provided by the Sinhala language, while yet introducing modes of expression, forms of language, and kinds of subject matter, which would enable the language to respond to the needs of a mass readership living in rapidly changing circumstances. Ortiz was perhaps especially well placed to articulate the particular challenge faced by late colonial and postcolonial intellectuals, because the circumstances of a former slave colony raised certain stark questions – especially the question of cultural origins – even as they closed off certain obvious responses. The impossible response was an appeal to a singular source of cultural authenticity, and what made this response impossible was the undeniable fact that 'the reflexive cultures and consciousness of the European settlers and those of the Africans they enslaved, the "Indians" they slaughtered, and the Asians they indentured were not, even in situations of the most extreme brutality, sealed off hermetically from each other' (Gilroy 1993: 2). Paul Gilroy's comment from the start of his own enquiry into the transnational world of the black Atlantic should remind us just how radical the approach of writers like Ortiz, Wickramasinghe, *and* Malinowski actually was, and why it should still matter to us today. The fiction of the separate, closed worlds of the 'native' and the 'settler' was a crucial part of the late colonial landscape, most familiar to us now in its late political flowering under South Africa's Apartheid regime. It is, though, a fiction that still haunts a great deal of anthropology, which until recently continued to work with unacknowledged canons of cultural authenticity which could silently filter out inauthentic signs of the modern from the ethnographic landscape.

The Nation and the Universal

In the next chapter I shall give rather more political substance to my argument by tracing an example of the local construal of an apparently familiar institutional procedure, the fate of electoral ritual in Sri Lanka. Before that, though, I want to return again to Ghosh's 'universal, irresistible metaphysic of modern meaning', and I want to do this initially through the case of the nation-state.

Partha Chatterjee's problem with the nation-state is spelt out forcefully at the start of his *The Nation and its Fragments*:

The result is that autonomous forms of imagination of the community were, and continue to be, overwhelmed and swamped by the history of the post-colonial state. Here lies the root of our postcolonial misery: not in our inability to think out new forms of the modern community but in our surrender to old forms of the modern state. If the nation is an imagined community and if nations must also take the form of states, then our theoretical language must allow us to talk about community and state at the same time. I do not think our present theoretical language allows us to do this. (Chatterjee 1993: 11)

I shall return to Chatterjee's understanding of state and community in chapter seven. The case behind this particular diagnosis of the failings of nationalism is made in Chatterjee's earlier book, *Nationalist Thought and the Colonial World* (Chatterjee 1986). The book combines a general theoretical argument about nationalism outside Europe with close reading of three key figures in the history of Indian nationalism: the nineteenth-century Bengali polymath, Bankim Chandra Chattopadhay, Gandhi, and Nehru.

Chatterjee starts with the same problem we have been pursuing throughout this chapter, only this time concerned not with institutions, or things to smoke and eat (like tobacco and sugar), but with political ideas. If nationalism is, as many commentators have argued, a political theory born in Europe at the end of the eighteenth and start of the nineteenth centuries, what then of anti-colonial, anti-European nationalisms: 'Nationalism sets out to assert its freedom from European domination. But in the very conception of its project, it remains a prisoner of the prevalent European intellectual fashions' (Chatterjee 1986: 10). *This* is the heart of Chatterjee's problem and, in answering it, he sets out a number of questions about the relationship between 'thought, culture, and power'. Most of these are broadly sociological. Do changes in ideas presuppose some change in the conditions of possibility in the wider society? How would a group of new thinkers attempt to change the habits of 'tradition'? The third question is most obviously relevant here:

Third, there is the question of the implantation into new cultures of categories and frameworks of thought produced in other – alien – cultural contexts. Is the positive knowledge contained in these frameworks neutral to the cultural context? Do they have different social consequences when projected on different socio-cultural conditions? Even more interestingly, do the categories and theoretical relations themselves acquire new meanings in their new cultural context? What then of the positivity of knowledge? (Chatterjee 1986: 27)

These are the same questions that were asked in my late colonial conversation, but Chatterjee's answers are very different from those of Ortiz, Malinowski, and Wickramasinghe, not least because of the third element in his bundle of issues – power. What happens to this question, he asks, when cultural difference maps on to a relation of dominance, as in colonial situations? And what of the internal power relations among the colonized?

Chatterjee's answer to these last two questions turns out to be rather a narrow one. It involves a series of identifications: nationalism is a product of post-Enlightenment social thought; post-Enlightenment social thought speaks in the name of Universal Reason; Reason and science divide time up into the time before Enlightenment and the time after Enlightenment, and divide the world into those who have achieved progress and modernity, and those others who have not. Reason thus requires its Other, and the colonial world furnishes it (Chatterjee 1986: 16–17). Chatterjee's argument here depends on his own enthusiastic reading of European poststructural social philosophers, of whom Foucault is clearly most important (Chatterjee 1986: 53 n. 18). It is also an argument which has been much more widely accepted amongst other postcolonial theorists – although few manage to match Chatterjee's power and lucidity. There is, though, an alternative way to construe the same story as intellectual history. This would position nationalist ideology within the Romantic reaction to the Enlightenment, what Isaiah Berlin called 'the counter-Enlightenment'. Its roots lie in writing like this (from the German Romantic philosopher Herder):

How much depth there is in the character of a single people, which, no matter how often observed (and gazed at with curiosity and wonder), nevertheless escapes the word which attempts to capture it, and, even with the word to catch it, is seldom so recognizable as to be universally understood and felt. If this is so, what happens when one tries to master an entire ocean of peoples, times, cultures, countries, with one glance, one sentiment, by means of one single word! Words, pale shadow-play! An entire living picture of ways of life, or habits, wants, characteristics of land and sky, must be added, or provided in advance; one must start by feeling sympathy with a nation if one is to feel a single one of its inclinations or acts, or all of them together. (Herder in Berlin 1976: 188)

The history of Western thought since the eighteenth century, in this version, is not the history of the uninterrupted march of Universal Reason, but is itself a much more contrapuntal tale, as the voices for science, industry, Reason, and the modern are met and matched by the countering voices for imagination and affect, art and the pre-industrial, culture and the *volk*: on one side Darwin, Spencer, and Comte, on the other Blake, Ruskin, and Tolstoy. A close reading of French poststructuralist theorists, or of Nietzsche, or Heidegger, does not enable one to jump out of the oppressive frame of post-Enlightenment thought: it instead allows one to take up a rather more familiar position *within* that broad and dissonant babble (cf. Hansen 1997).

In Chatterjee's analysis of his three nationalist thinkers he employs a further distinction, separating out what he calls the 'problematic' from the 'thematic' in their speeches and writings. The distinction for Chatterjee roughly corresponds to the claims asserted in an ideology, and the principles (moral, epistemological, etc.) used to justify it. So Bankim, the nineteenth-century Bengali, had for his 'problematic', various aspects of Indian society and culture; but for his 'thematic' he referred back to the canons of nineteenth-century science and rationality. Nehru was even more wedded to the thematic of European Reason, as he tried to make of the newly independent India a modern industrial society based on central state planning. Only Gandhi refused to be drawn into the thematic of rationality, explicitly justifying his decisions and public statements with reference not to science but to religion, and vehemently arguing against the idea of a postcolonial India with a powerful state committed to progress and industry. Of my earlier examples, Wickramasinghe, with his insouciant confidence in the possibility of blending the indigenous and the scientific, would undoubtedly fail the thematic test too.

What is happening here is akin to the analytic structure developed by Guha, and discussed in the previous chapter. A model is constructed for the interaction of the indigenous and the colonial. Like Guha, Chatterjee presents the state as external, an avatar of European rationality at its most coercive, and insists on the possibility of analytically separating the derivative from the non-derivative ('authentic' seems the obvious antonym) in his examples of nationalist thought. In his later book, he employs another dichotomy, between the 'outer' and 'inner', the public world of state and law, and the home life of spirit and culture, in order to make the important argument that in India the work of nationalist resistance was first advanced in the intimate spaces of 'culture', and only later ventured into contestation in the outer world of the colonial political order (Chatterjee 1993).

What, though, of Chatterjee's question about 'the implantation into new cultures of categories and frameworks of thought produced in other – alien – cultural contexts'? In its framing, and in some of his later writing, it would seem to imply the possibility that colonial science and colonial administration might be reinterpreted, appropriated, made somehow Indian. Certainly it would be relatively easy to find plausible historical evidence to support this possibility. But more often, there seems to be some special ontological weight credited to European rationality in his argument, which makes it an unbending and unblending thing of implacable hardness. As Dipesh Chakrabarty puts it

Concepts such as citizenship, the state, civil society, public sphere, human rights, equality before the law, the individual, distinctions between public and private, the idea of the subject, democracy, popular sovereignty, social justice, scientific rationality, and soon all bear the burden of European thought and history... These concepts entail an unavoidable – and in a sense inescapable – universal and secular vision of the human. (Chakrabarty 2000: 4)

Chakrabarty's genealogical point is transformed into something stronger in a recent piece by David Scott:

I want to inquire into what appears to me a problem in the now considerably advanced discussion about colonialism – a problem that turns very much on the question of what is distinctive about the political rationality of forms of power, on the one hand, and on the other, on those transformations effected by *modern* power, the consequence of which is that the old, premodern possibilities are not only no longer conceptually approachable except in the languages of the modern, but are now no longer available as practical historical options. (Scott 1999: 23; cf. Scott 1995)

This takes the argument one step further: modern, rational – read 'colonial' – power makes it impossible to think in terms of other, older political possibilities; it also removes them as practical options for action. We have arrived at Ghosh's 'irreversible triumph of the language that had usurped all the others in which people once discussed their differences'.

But have we? The argument in this part of the chapter has been untroubled by attention to what Indians, Sri Lankans, or anyone else not from the professorial class, say about the state, difference, politics, and community. In the rest of this book I will try to redress the balance, and in so doing query this curious intellectual capitulation to the 'irreversible triumph' of the single language of political modernity. In the course of this chapter, we have also gradually moved away from the concern with institutions, practices, and material objects, towards theoretical issues to do with the translatability of more or less theoretical concepts and sytems.[5]

One word which has not yet featured in this discussion, but which poses special problems for the argument put forward by Chatterjee and Ghosh, is 'democracy'. Whatever the reasons, and whatever the implications, the institutions of representative democracy have become deeply socially embedded in India and Sri Lanka, to the extent that some recent commentators even speak of a 'Tocquevillian revolution' in India (Kaviraj 1998; Hansen 1999). But none of the available evidence suggests that this has been accompanied by the magical transformation of Indians and Sri Lankans *en masse* into liberal political subjects. In the next chapter I will look at one local case of democracy in practice, in order to tease out what this revolution may or may not imply, and also to make a case for the development of a more thorough-going anthropology of democracy and its attendant spaces for staging the political.

Coda: The Political Afterlife of Culture

The writers I have discussed in this chapter deserve a fuller account than I have provided here, and my version is undoubtedly biassed towards the kind of story I am trying to tell in this book. By way of caution, I should close the chapter with a note or two from the other, darker side of the same conversation. There are, of course, other ways of reading my three conversationalists. I have already mentioned Gluckman's impatience with Malinowski's writing on culture change in Africa, which included the occasional defence of the colonial status quo, in

---

[5] Even Scott's analysis, which I have just quoted, is based on his reading of an edited volume of colonial administrative proposals from the early nineteenth century (Mendis 1956). Scott deconstructs what he sees as their political implications, but is apparently unconcerned with what happened to those proposals once – or even, *if* – they were instituted in colonial practice.

which he reserves his greatest scorn for some spectacular toadying to the authorities on Malinowski's part ('the anthropologist crawling on his knees to beg some White groups for a few more crumbs for the Africans' (Gluckman 1949: 10)). Ortiz's earlier writings are now found by some to contain unacceptable traces of racism (Davies 2000: 162–3 n. 13). And Wickramasinghe, in a lecture to students in the year Sri Lanka first burst into flames, combined a reiteration of his anthropological influences with a passionate defence of a more narrowly conceived vision of traditional culture, which for him meant the culture of rural Sinhala Buddhists (Wickramasinghe 1975 [1971]).

Wickramasinghe's successors as writers and critics in Sri Lanka have mostly turned their back on his anthropological enthusiasms, preferring instead to work over this more familiar ground of 'traditional culture', itself now posited in a more straightforwardly oppositional relationship to 'the West' and modernity in general. So, for example, the novelist Gunadasa Amarasekera, in some respects an equivalent literary figure to Wickramasinghe in contemporary Sri Lanka, has claimed that modernity 'has been imposed on us and as such it is emotionally and spiritually an alien world for us Asians. Emotionally and spiritually we live in our traditional world' (Nanayakkara 2004: 13). For Amarasekera, there is no attraction in a project of creative borrowing: the modern must instead be resisted. He is a senior member of a prominent grouping of literary and academic figures in Sri Lanka, who combine a hard-line on the ethnic question, with reflections on the threats to indigenous culture. Their enemies are many, but anthropologists figure prominently in the nationalist demonology. The remarkable generation of Sri Lankan anthropologists who came to prominence in the 1960s and 1970s, who we could think of as Wickramasinghe's children (not their choice of epithet I concede), and whose best work exemplifies that dynamic sense of culture in the making that I have traced in Ortiz's classic (Tambiah 1976; Obeyesekere 1981; Seneviratne 1999), now find themselves demonized at home as 'anti-national' elements by their chauvinist enemies.

In December 2005 the biennial International Sri Lanka Studies Conference included a panel with the title 'The New Missionary Position: Current Anthropology of Sri Lanka as an Ideology for Re-Colonization'. Its abstract included the following:

Sri Lankan anthropology unlike in other countries did not go through a decolonization process and slipped easily into a virulent colonial mode. It has given rise to a semi-fictional school of anthropology studies. Here, local reality is deeply misread and it's [*sic*] mostly Buddhist subjects of study continually derided. The result is a large body of literature on Sinhalese Buddhists, tangential to truth which has set in a train of socially solipsistic citations, especially by foreign anthropologists, strangers to the local culture coming here for a relatively short time. These studies have also denounced the local anti-colonial renaissance and thus implicitly hanker after the colonial period. Echoing colonial missionaries, these writers have also continuously called for foreign intervention in the country.[6]

The convenor of the panel was Susantha Goonatilake, a minor figure on the international postcolonial science circuit, but a high-profile Sinhala nationalist in Sri Lanka. In the early 1990s, Goonatilake was prominently involved in the campaign which led to the banning in Sri Lanka of Stanley Tambiah's *Buddhism Betrayed* (Tambiah 1992), and which he has now extended into a wider (and wilder) critique of all postcolonial anthropology in the country (Goonatilake 2001). Reading Goonatilake's splenetic attacks on my colleagues, it is hard not to think we must be doing something right to warrant this level of attention. But in the face of this apparently 'irreversible triumph' of the language of cultural difference, it is all the more important to keep alive the more open possibilities exemplified in the exchanges across continents in my late colonial conversation.

---

[6] Panel abstract, 10th Sri Lankan Studies Conference, Kelaniya December 2005: http://www.kln.ac.lk/10thicsls/10thicslspanels.html, accessed 13 December 2005.

FOUR

Performing Democracy

The most exciting recent writing on democracy in South Asia has come on the boundary between political theory, history and anthropology. In his wonderful overview of India in the years since Independence, Sunil Khilnani pays particular attention to the place of democracy and the state in India's social fabric:

Democracy is a type of government, a political regime of laws and institutions. But its imaginative potency rests in its promise to bring alien and powerful machines like the state under the control of human will, to enable a community of political equals before the constitutional law to make their own history. Like those other great democratic experiments inaugurated in eighteenth-century America and France, India became a democracy without really knowing how, why, or what it meant to be one. Yet the democratic idea has penetrated the Indian political imagination and has begun to corrode the authority of the social order and of a paternalist state. Democracy as a manner of seeing and acting upon the world is changing the relation of Indians to themselves. (Khilnani 1997: 16–17)

And Thomas Hansen places democracy and its consequences at the heart of his important study of the rise of Hindu nationalism. He follows Sudipta Kaviraj (1998) in discerning a strange kind of 'Tocquevillian revolution' in post-Independence India:

3 'Vote for this' (Communist slogan, West Bengal)

[Not] because India represents a replay of the western democratic revolutions or because democracy always tends towards the production of modern individuals and citizenship, as a more conventional Tocquevillean thesis would run. I would argue, quite the contrary, that the idea of a democratic revolution in India makes sense exactly because the trajectory of modernity and democracy in India demonstrates so clearly how democracy makes the political dimensions of society crucial, productive, and deeply problematic. (Hansen 1999: 57)

These formulations, if at all true, raise genuinely exciting empirical questions: democracy as a corrosive force 'changimg the relation of Indians to themselves'; the emergence of 'the political' as something 'crucial, productive, and deeply problematic'. They also potentially transform the terms of the argument we examined in the previous chapter, for they suggest something rather more than either of the apparent alternatives: neither the purely local appropriation and interpretation of modern political institutions; nor the 'irreversible triumph' of the language of political modernity. Rather, we have to find ways to analyse and describe democracy and the political as a force that has the potential to transform other areas of life, but not in any particular or predictable way. It is a force characterized by what Hansen, paraphrasing the French political philosopher Claude Lefort, has called a spirit of 'ubiquitous contingency' (Hansen 1999: 57).

In this respect the anthropological contribution to the analysis of democracy has been rather disappointing. 'Democracy' as an object of study in its own right is all but invisible in Vincent's *Anthropology and Politics* (Vincent 1990), and while her more recent co-edited *Companion to the Anthropology of Politics* finds room for essays on topics as various as 'Citizenship', 'Neoliberalism', 'Displacement', and 'Genetic Citizenship' (among many others), there is no essay on 'Democracy', and a mere three entries under that word in the Index (Nugent and Vincent 2004). There are a number of possible explanations, some overlapping. It could be that anthropologists see 'democracy' as no more than an ideological chimera – an imaginary *telos* to justify Western military adventures in other parts of the world. (There is no chapter on 'Terrorism' either in the Nugent and Vincent volume, although it does have rather more hits in the Index.) It could be that democracy's very ubiquity in modern political arrangements renders it banal as an object for anthropological analysis. Or it could be that the recent political turn in ethnography reproduces the biases of its main theoretical inspirations: Foucault's political trajectory, for example, was inspired by his break with the authoritarian hold of the French Communist Party, but he seems to have carried over their contemptuous dismissal of 'bourgeois democracy', preferring to align himself with extreme ultra-left groups, or more often, with no one at all. Politically more imaginative French social critics – like Claude Lefort, with his roots in the *Socialisme ou barbarie* group (Lefort 1986; Lefort 1988) – remain almost unknown to most anthropologists. Yet Lefort's argument for the 'radical indeterminacy' engendered by democracy provides as compelling an object for anthropological enquiry as any I know of, while

4 'I can do anything' (J. R. Jayawardene at Presidential election rally, Sri Lanka 1992)

the empirical evidence for everyday engagement with democratic institutions in all parts of the world is quite simply overwhelming.

But if there is to be an anthropology of democracy, what kind of object do we take 'democracy' to be? One approach, exemplified in the recent work of Julia Paley (Paley 2002; Paley 2004), systematically examines the gap between the promise of popular decision-making and the stark reality of disempowerment and exclusion. For all its obvious strengths, I find this work hugs too closely to the normative contours of the democratic project: all the while, the implicit question seems to be, 'But is this *real* democracy?' A second, more promising, departure is to concentrate on the technology of democracy – the rituals, procedures, and material culture of the ballot – in the hope that the cold stare of the ethnographic eye will defamiliarize what is, when all is said and done, a quite odd practice (Coles 2004; Pels *et al.* 2007). A third is to assess the cultural implications of democratic procedures and ideas as they are received in different contexts. West's recent depiction of unruly democracy in Mozambique, for example, seems to illustrate beautifully Lefort's notion of 'radical contingency': as someone tells him, confronted with the violence and destabilization that follows the introduction of electoral democracy, 'with democracy, anything can be said and anything can be done' (West 2005: 29).

Elections and Performances

If democracy can be defined as the idea 'that in human political communities it ought to be ordinary people . . . and not extra-ordinary people who rule' (Dunn 1992: v), elections are the principal means whereby ordinary people remind themselves that, whatever the appearances to the contrary (and they are usually many and various), 'they' are in charge of their own destiny. As John Dunn put it in the context of an analysis of an election in Ghana: 'Elections are events which confuse in a very intimate and purposeful way the largely symbolic identifications of large numbers of people with their effects upon the politically effective conduct of rather small numbers of people. Such confusion is indeed their point' (Dunn 1980: 112). Modern democracies hinge on the idea of representation, of one person standing for a much larger group of people, making the decisions 'they' might expect to make had they been consulted. And the mysterious link between representative and represented is established and renewed in ritual form: through elections.

The idea that elections are best understood as ritual (rather than, or as much as, instrumental) actions is itself a reasonably familiar one. In the analysis of a West African election which I have just quoted, Dunn mentions in passing American research which claimed to establish that, on purely instrumental grounds, there was insufficient at stake for the average citizen of a Western democracy to bother to vote at all (Dunn 1980: 137). As Edelman puts it early in his influential *The Symbolic Uses of*

Politics, 'what people get does not depend mainly on their votes' (Edelman 1985: 3). Like other commentators, Edelman stresses the legitimacy that the whole political system enjoys as a result of popular participation in electoral ritual. He goes further, though, in claiming that this legitimacy crucially depends on the electorate continuing to misapprehend their rituals of agency, which in practice are of little significance to actual decision-making, as genuinely momentous choices which will inevitably affect the lives of the whole political community. Steven Lukes makes a similar point that elections express 'the symbolic affirmation of the voters' acceptance of the political system and of their role within it' (Lukes 1975: 304). But, in keeping with the whole thrust of his critique of Durkheimian approaches to political ritual, Lukes also points out that electoral rituals can also be interpreted as part of the hegemonic apparatus by which a particular political system reproduces itself, by 'defining away' alternative understandings of political possibility (Lukes 1975: 305).

Writers like Lukes and Dunn and Edelman are correct to point to the importance of elections as rituals of participation or legitimation. Nevertheless, in their comments on elections, there is a residual hint of the 'mere ritual' approach to the symbolic, in which the illusion of ritual masks the reality of politics proper. This may be justified when we compare the practical consequences of voters' decisions with the practical consequences of politicians' decisions. But in keeping with a whole trend in anthropological studies of ritual, I think we should try to avoid separating off the ritual superstructure from some underlying social structural or political base. Instead we should treat rituals as *sui generis*, as particular forms of life, with their own causes and consequences which cannot and should not be reduced to some supposedly more mundane and therefore 'realer' area of social life. To take a classic example from another area of anthropology, Maurice Bloch and Jonathan Parry argue that mortuary rituals do not provide an occasion for 'society' to respond to death, but rather the rituals themselves provide 'an occasion for *creating* that "society" as an apparently external force'(Bloch and Parry 1982: 6). So too, elections, like other so-called political rituals, are not epiphenomenal to the world of real politics. Rather they are crucial sites for the production and reproduction of the political.

If we accord elections a moral value in their own right, then the import of an election in people's lives can be at least as significant as the import of any of the subsequent actions of those elected. Elections are also dramas of identity and difference, based upon the affirmation of moral identifications amongst 'us' and the drawing of equally moral differentiations from 'them'. And in choosing a representative, electors do not merely choose an identification for themselves, they also have occasion to contemplate an odd symbolic paradox: the person who embodies that identification has not only to be utterly the same as 'us', she also has to be at once somehow and mysteriously different enough to act as a voice for us and a reliable embodiment of our collective agency.

In this chapter I want to approach these issues through a single case-study: an account of a national election as experienced by a village in Sri Lanka in the early 1980s. But I have chosen to describe the election not in terms of leaders and factions, vertical and horizontal ties, but instead in terms of ritual and spectacle. Political ritual has been something of an embarrassment to political anthropology (and even more so to political science). As a topic it is clearly important, self-evidently spectacular, but apart from mere description, there seems a problem about what else to say about it. One reason is the spectre of functionalism that hovers so low over the study of political ritual: what we most often ask about political ritual is 'what does it *do*?' – bring in voters, restore central values, reassure the powerful, reassure the powerless, act as a safety-valve? In each case the answer is sought outside the ritual itself in some more tangible and 'real' area of social life. I want to start with something different, a shocking tautology – political ritual produces something we can call 'the political'. I shall try to enlarge on this superficially unimpressive formula later in this chapter.

Voting as a Moral Phenomenon

The inferno reaches its climax, of course, on election day when luxurious limousines flying the colours of the various candidates or those of their parties, drive up under my portico to take me to the polling station. My refusal to accept any of these offers has a curious result: every party thinks I am on the other side and, whoever wins, I have to endure the hoots and jeers of the victor's supporters as they pass my gates. (Bandaranaike 1963 [1954]: 467)

By the time I started my first fieldwork there in the early 1980s, electoral politics in Sri Lanka had become a central ritual arena within which all sorts of moral dramas of purely local import were acted out. As the quotation from a light-hearted piece of journalism by S. W. R. D. Bandaranaike (the politician whose brief period of power in the 1950s was based on the first mass mobilization in the name of Sinhala nationalism) shows, some of this was already well established in the years immediately after Independence. In Sri Lanka elections have provided a ritual idiom within which people can express their visions of moral community and moral order. Or as Richard Gombrich's neighbours in Sri Lanka in the 1960s put it more succinctly in a song they taught to their children, 'Our colour is green, We are not rowdies.' Green is the party colour of Sri Lanka's United National Party; Gombrich's neighbours told him that the problem with their political opponents was that they 'scolded too much' (Gombrich 1971: 266).

One point, then, is that party identification at elections is often justified by appeal to moral criteria: we are good people, they are bad people. A second is that elections imply division within a community into 'our' side and 'their' side. This inescapable division has been a source of recurring anxiety in widely different areas of Sinhala life. For example, when Buddhist monks are elected to positions of authority in the *sangha*, it is customary to represent the winner as an uncontested victor by unanimous acclaim. In fact, such a decision is preceded by a great deal of hard, behind-the-scenes politicking, but this is always hidden from public view so as to allow the *sangha* to maintain a public front of undivided unity (Kemper 1991: 212). That is one solution to the moral dilemmas of electoral ritual, and I will return to this figure of 'unity' and its embodiment in Buddhism later, but for now I want only to make one further point. Not only are political divisions themselves justified in terms of 'good' and 'bad' people, the very existence of political division is frequently seen as 'bad' in contrast to the widespread ideal of unity and unanimity.

Let me now describe some of the circumstances in my fieldwork that first provoked this line of enquiry (Spencer 1990b). I arrived in the village I have called Tenna in April 1982. The village had a population of over 1,000, mostly Sinhala Buddhists but with a number of Tamil-speaking Muslim families clustered around a Muslim shrine on one side of the village. Most of the population were newcomers, rural migrants who had settled (like many others in post-Independence Sri Lanka) on areas of unused Crown land. The village elite, such as they were, were the core group of farmers and minor officials who owned and worked the village's small acreage of paddy-land. The migrants made their living as best they could from combinations of day-labour, gemming, vegetable cash-cropping, and various other marginal economic activities.

The village was in a particularly interesting political location. It was in an area which had been dominated during the colonial period by one or two high-caste families, landlords and colonial officials. One of those families had married into a Colombo-based family from the highest ranks of the indigenous elite. Village sharecroppers in the 1980s still set aside shares of the harvest for ex-cabinet ministers and a former Prime Minister from the family of the village's old landlords. Ironically, this family dominated the left-of-centre Sri Lanka Freedom Party (SLFP), allowing its ostensibly right-of-centre opponents in the UNP to pose locally as populist opponents of the old 'feudal' lords. From 1956, the village had been part of a constituency which faithfully returned SLFP MPs from the family of the old landlords. In 1977 this all changed when the SLFP government was voted out of office in a landslide national victory for the UNP; locally the sitting SLFP MP was replaced by a local Muslim landowner representing the UNP. I could continue in this vein, but the point I want to make is straightforward: local political alignments were complex, and, in particular, ethnic and class factors were hopelessly tangled in the contingencies of local political history, such that the right-wing party represented itself as the party of the little people, while the left-wing party represented itself as the party of the majority Buddhist community.

The change in the village in 1977 was traumatic for some. The handful of richer families who dominated village politics were predominantly identified with the SLFP, while the new powers of the UNP were associated with a group of younger incomers, who proceeded to assert their power over the distribution of jobs and contracts and favours with the police and local officials. But the displaced SLFP supporters bided their time, secure in the knowledge that in every previous election in the previous quarter-century the ruling party had been voted out after a single term. Their time would surely come again.

By April 1982 that time was fast approaching as the date for elections drew closer. The UNP government had introduced a new constitution in 1978, concentrating power in the hands of an executive Presidency and replacing the existing first-past-the-post electoral system with a system based on proportional representation. Both the President and MPs were due to be tested at the polls within the next twelve months.

Not that any of this would have been guessed by a naïve observer of a village like Tenna in the summer of 1982. For the first six months of my stay, the village managed collectively to beguile me with a convincing and frustrating display of unity and amity. On arrival I was placed in a room at the village temple by various of the village worthies (who turned a deaf ear to my pleas to be allowed instead to lodge with an 'ordinary' family). From there I was well placed to observe a whole series of rituals of village unity, centred on the school and the temple, dominated by the symbolism of Sinhala Buddhist nationalism, and orchestrated by younger members of the village's politically central families. Once a month on the full-moon day, chanting schoolchildren would march around the village and into the temple to take part in a collective offering to the Buddha. In July and August these processions were stepped up for the season of the monastic retreat (*vas*), while the big full-moon days also involved loudspeakers and rituals, a play of numbing piety written and performed by villagers, and collective offerings of alms to the *sangha*.

These large public displays of village amity were complemented by equally telling small encounters with villagers, all smiling amicably and treating me with a frustrating *politesse*. Even the children seemed preternaturally pacific in their games with each other. It was, as I have suggested, enormously charming. It was also, for a fieldworker anxious about the doctoral thesis which would have to be spun out of such apparently bland material, often painfully boring. In retrospect, I find occasional clues in my notes to what was about to break over me. A minor government official asked me whether I was interested in 'politics', and immediately interrupted himself to announce that I could not possibly be, because politics was a 'bad' area, and all that I would find there was 'trouble'. In August I attended a political rally organized by the opposition in the nearest town and noticed a lot of threatening-looking young men standing around on the fringes. I was surprised when I returned to be greeted by the matter-of-fact enquiry, 'How much trouble was there?' and equally surprised when my interlocutor looked sceptical at my assurance that the meeting had passed peacefully.

But it was in September that my unnatural calm was shattered irrevocably. In early September it was announced that the country's first Presidential election was to be held in October. A few days later the village branch of the ruling party organized a rally which was addressed by the sitting MP. A few days after that, I was watching yet another pious procession making its way to the village temple when suddenly there was a flurry of shouting and fists. Someone, a young man close to the village

UNP leadership, had attacked one of the men leading the procession. Various respected figures – a schoolteacher and the village headman – attempted to intercede. 'Just wait', the young man shouted defiantly, 'until the day of the election. We'll see you transferred far away (into the Tamil areas of the country).' And then he was led away by friends, still muttering angrily.

The rest of the evening at the temple was spent in tense discussion as the leaders of the temple committee decided how they should best respond to what they saw as an outrageous assault on a peaceful religious procession. The explanations I was offered from members of the committee were all variations on the theme I quoted from Gombrich's neighbours. These people – the young man and his friends in the UNP – are bad people; they are troublemakers; they drink and start fights. The young man in particular was criticized for his general lack of *lajja*, that central value of shame and constraint which is so highly valued in Sinhala public encounters.

In my earlier book, *A Sinhala Village in a Time of Trouble* (Spencer 1990b), I use this moment of contrast – the restrained Buddhist ritual interrupted by the (possibly) drunken outburst – to illuminate at least two salient areas of village life. On the one hand it represented the contradiction between the ideal of unity, as expressed in the village's identity as a village of Sinhala Buddhists, and thus part of the greater collectivity of the Sinhala Buddhist nation, and the reality of party political division which split the village into two, often hostile, groups. But it also represented a slightly different sort of contrast, between the *politesse*, restraint, and gentleness of everyday public life as I had witnessed it so far, and the rowdy, aggressive turmoil of village politics.

Over the next few months I had plenty of opportunity to witness this sea-change in the moral texture of everyday life. A year later, as I was preparing to leave Tenna, a friend confided to me that, in my first months in the village, he and his fellow villagers had been concerned that I should only see the good side of the village, and so they had tried to screen me from expressions of animosity and discord. From the moment of the attack at the temple such screening was impossible. Instead of avoiding comment on the failings of their neighbours, my friends and informants started to tell me more and more about their minor wickednesses and past misdeeds. Instead of a sense of preternatural gentleness, I was now struck by the tension and air of barely contained aggression in public encounters.

It is always difficult to justify this kind of interpretation of a shift in the public mood, but I was certainly not alone in sensing a change in the village. During the election I was again and again reassured that the current unseemly state of village affairs was purely temporary, it was because of 'politics' (*desapalanaya*), and when the election was over the trouble would end and all would return to normal. During those months the village was also occupied by a parallel ritual drama, a case of spirit possession involving a young Muslim woman who found herself possessed, interestingly enough, by a host of Buddhist demons (Spencer 1997a). Some interpreted the possession itself as a symptom of the moral danger the village had fallen into because of the election. As public tension mounted on the eve of the election itself the daily chanting of Buddhist protective verses (*pirit*) which had been going on at her house was suspended. I asked her neighbours why this was so and was told that because of politics, people's minds were 'bad', and for the verses to work they had to be chanted by people in a state of mental purity. In short, the election had induced a state of collective moral disorder.

Excursus: The Passions and the Interests

My assessment of village politics as I encountered them in Sri Lanka in the early 1980s ran counter to the prevailing wisdom, both local and academic. The orthodoxy was that the introduction of party politics had 'split' villages, believed to have been previously harmonious and united (see, e.g., Robinson 1975). My view was that if party politics had not come to the village, the villagers would have had to invent them. Politics had simply provided a new idiom in which villagers could express the kinds of division that had long existed. As such, electoral politics was simply the latest in a line of institutions which villagers had appropriated for their own uses. In the colonial and immediate postcolonial period, what we might call purely personal disputes were conducted through the colonial courts and through complaints and petitions to local officials. Colonial civil servants and judges were dismayed by what they saw as this abuse of the legal system by pathologically 'litigious' peasants. What was happening was that peasants were appropriating the machinery of the colonial state as a means to conduct their own local, 'private' arguments about standing and status.

In the 1950s and early 1960s, when ethnographers like Leach (1961) and Obeyesekere (1967) carried out their fieldwork in rural Sri Lanka, the main focus of village disputes was access to land. But what is interesting about these disputes is that in many cases the cost of pursuing the dispute far outweighed the potential economic benefit of the land that was being fought over. Arguments about land, I have argued elsewhere, were as much arguments about membership of the village as a moral community, as they were arguments about access to material resources (Spencer 1990b). In the late colonial period the local courts were, for many, the privileged space for agonistic engagement. Twenty or thirty years later, I heard almost no talk of land disputes (although the kinds of case discussed by Leach and Obeyesekere had existed in the past), for two reasons. One was that there were just too many people in the village for land rights to be used as a way of talking about membership in the moral community of the village. The other was that people could use politics for this purpose instead.

The analogy with land disputes allows to me to deal with the objection that almost every Sri Lankan colleague has made to my argument. Politics is not about morality, it is about resources. Village politics are all about patronage, about getting government jobs and loans, contracts and favours. This is how villagers see politics, and few analysts would disagree with them. I have a number of qualifications to make to this interpretation. One is that a successful patronage system does not require two-party competition, of the sort I found so entrenched in Sri Lankan villages. Second, many of the resources distributed by the state (health and education services, for example) are too general to be suitable for targeting to political followers. Finally, far more people enthusiastically take part in public politics (or did in the early 1980s) than could ever hope to benefit from the handful of government jobs that were available as spoils to the victors.

None of which should be taken as dismissing the real material benefits people could gain from political activity. The local UNP leaders had prospered greatly from the fruits of office, while the vanquished SLFP members were keenly aware of the obstacles that stood between them and government employment, for example. And local politicians strove valiantly to present every last appearance of state support as a personal boon which they personally had brought to the area. But what I think the village interpretation of politics as material self-interest really means was that politics had become the area of life within which egoistic displays of naked self-interest were not merely expected, they were in a sense also produced. In village conversations, 'politics' was used as a convenient catch-all explanation for all manner of egoistic and anti-social behaviour: it's not entirely our fault, people seemed to be saying, it was politics that made us act this way.

All of this was clearly visible in the complex and murky contingencies of local political affiliation. As far as public political alignment was concerned – gauged by attendance at rallies and the display of posters – it was more or less impossible to assign any sociological coherence to the supporters of either of the two parties in the election. Both contained both rich and poor, low and high castes. (The sole exception were the Muslims who seemed solid behind their MP.) Instead I uncovered sinuous tales of individual and family animosities: this farmer's family had been SLFP supporters since the 1950s; his neighbour went over to the UNP a few years ago after a dispute over damage caused by the farmer's buffaloes; and so on. Which came first, personal dispute or party-based opposition, was usually impossible to tell.

If we had to sum up the political conundrum confronted by these villagers in 1982 it was this: how to reconcile the widely shared sense of the importance of unity and community as over-riding values with a style of politics, culturally defined as the absence of unity and the temporary loss of community. And the historical tragedy the country was quietly slipping into in the early 1980s also emerged from the style of politics I have been describing. Briefly, politics mattered too much. What was at stake in local political divisions was a dangerous mixture of thwarted (or satisfied) material interest combined with a constantly bubbling sense of moral outrage. The tragedy of the youth uprising of the late 1980s, in which thousands of young people 'disappeared', is explicable as a continuation and development of the kind of politics I witnessed in the early 1980s.

Politics as a Public Phenomenon

How did these themes appear in the public performances that marked the build-up to the elections? The political rallies held in the area during the election provide good examples. The rallies are extremely important as public rituals. Every village had several such rallies in the course of the campaign, usually addressed by local politicians and occasionally by village political leaders. The rally would last for an hour or two and would be attended by anything between 40 and 100 supporters. To mark the occasion, banners would be hung across the road and the area around the rally would be decorated with the party colours, blue for the SLFP, green for the UNP.

The rallies in the local town repeated these details, only on the grand scale. Coloured decorations would line the road for miles leading into and out of the town, which would itself be decked in banners and flags in the appropriate party colours. The rally itself was altogether more ambitious:

national politicians alternated with local speakers, movie stars, and popular singers. The stage from which this all emanated would also hold anything up to several hundred guests. Prominent on any platform would be a large group of Buddhist monks, sitting passively to one side as the speakers and singers entertained the crowd (Figure 4). And that is another point about rural politics: they were enormously entertaining. Political rallies, even outside election times, were the biggest regular public spectacles and often drew crowds in the tens of thousands, even in an area like this where the largest town had a population of little more than 10,000. And their appeal was also aesthetic: people would listen attentively, and comment approvingly or disapprovingly on the 'beauty' (*lassana*) of different speakers' oratory, regardless of their own political affiliation. In his vivid novel about the 1971 Insurrection, E. R. Sarachchandra describes a scene on the campus of Peradeniya University as a huge crowd of students were held spell-bound for hours by the oratory of the radical leader Rohana Wijeweera. It is the same year and the same setting as the lecture by Wickramasinghe with which I closed the last chapter:

The professor climbed out of his car and stood at the top of the bowl and looked down at Wijeweera. The man spoke without any of the histrionics of the usual political speaker, standing still with his legs slightly astride and his hands folded behind his back. He neither stamped his feet on the ground nor waved his fists in the air. An unbroken stream of words flowed out of his mouth in a rasping monotone as he dealt with historical, economic and political factors, pausing only to take a sip of water from a glass that was on the table that was in front of him. Professor Amaradasa listened for a while and then found that his attention was wandering from the speaker to the audience seated in a semi-circle around him. It was a marvel to see how they sat, the upper part of their bodies as still as statues, hanging on to every syllable that fell from the speaker's lips. (Sarachchandra 1978: 43)

How, we may ask, can we separate the political from the aesthetic, the ideological from the performative, in a description like this? It is especially telling that the author, as well as a sometime Professor at Peradeniya, is also Sri Lanka's leading post-Independence dramatist, and the setting for the speech is the open-air theatre on campus now named after him.

The tension between unity and egoism manifested itself in different politicians' styles. The incumbent President favoured a regal style, strong on that ostentatiously Buddhist set of public virtues he labelled *dharmista*. Listening to him speak I was impressed, more than anything, by how little he said, and in particular by the way he avoided the 'harsh' (*sära*) and 'scolding' speech of some other politicians. His Prime Minister, in marked contrast, was more of a street-fighter, and his speech (at a later rally) was altogether rougher and tougher, concentrating on vindictive and abuse aimed at his political opponents. As a team, the pair embodied a kind of diarchy, each representing one pole in this contrast between politics and community. Similarly, the local MP adopted a relatively mild and benign oratorical style, leaving the tougher and nastier speeches to his local election agent.

As far as the content of political oratory was concerned, the tension was explicit in the shift from appeals to positive images of unity and community, nearly always based on the key symbols of Sinhala Buddhist nationalism, to negative attacks on the behaviour, morality, and, occasionally, policies of their opponents. The positive concentrated on impersonal and relatively abstract symbols, the negative on specific and personal attacks. The spectator could see the contrast in the passive presence of the Buddhist monks on the platform, embodying the historic destiny of the Sinhala people as protectors of Buddhism, and the all too active shouting and gesticulating of the various political speakers. As in the oddities of the uncontested monkly election, Buddhist monks were effective as players in party politics just so long as they were not seen to be too obviously playing party politics. So, for all their role as backstage wheeler-dealers, in public they tended to avoid being drawn into unseemly displays of political egoism. Silence and stillness were the safest symbols of Buddhist unity.

The final public performance of the election, though, abandoned this tension between unity and egoism, in favour of a straightforward reversal of everyday values. This was the day of the voting itself, followed by the day in which the village listened *en masse* as the results came in on the radio, in which the carnivalesque aspects of the election became most inescapable. The voting for the Presidential election was in fact carried out with some decorum. Many voters dressed in their best clothes and went to the polls as whole families, sometimes at carefully calculated astrologically auspicious times. The turnout in the village was very high, at least as high as the national figure of 80 per cent, and probably nearer 90 per cent. The only mildly unsavoury aspect of the proceedings was the group of young men gathered at the UNP leader's house in the centre of the village who jeered their opponents as they passed on the way to vote at the village school.

The following day, though, was quite different. The first results were announced in the early morning and it soon became apparent, as each district declared, that the President had won convincingly. The group of supporters gathered at the UNP leader's house grew all morning, entertained with large amounts of dubious illicit liquor. Known SLFP supporters, fearing the worst, kept to their houses. As each result came in, the singing and chanting grew in volume as the victory party got drunker and drunker. In mid-afternoon, the village's only car, an ancient Peugeot, was pushed out and coaxed into reluctant life. With drunken UNP supporters sitting on its roof and bonnet, it led a large and erratic procession up and down the main road that ran through the village, sometimes chanting UNP slogans, at other times stopping outside the houses of known political opponents to shout more personalized insults. Back in the centre of the village, the crowd started dancing in the street, and the UNP leader himself hitched up his sarong to lead the revels. In this moment of extreme licence we had travelled a long way from the dull constraint and gentle politesse that had so frustrated me a month or two earlier.

After Politics

I have already indicated the debt I owed, in my original interpretation of village politics, to the literature on rites of reversal. The crowds outside the houses, taunting and abusing, recall the charivari of early modern Europe, the famous moments of licence in African rites of kingship, and the bawdy pleasures of Bakhtin's (1984) 'material bodily lower stratum'. The temptation, then, was to interpret all this in terms of a safely functional homeostasis. Year after year, the village would go its quiet, restrained way, then a couple of times a decade, all would be briefly reversed, the pent-up tensions would be released, only for order swiftly to reassert itself, all the stronger for the brief moment of reversal and licence. And the pattern of Sri Lankan politics from the 1950s to the early 1980s seemed to support this, as every sitting government was voted out of power in successive elections in what became known (in allusion to a form of rotating land tenure) as the political *tattumaru* system. Except, as in other rites of reversal, there is every reason to think that the moment of licence was as likely to create tension as dissipate it, while not all the attacks were symbolic or verbal. Post-election violence grew as a problem from the 1950s on, reaching a peak in 1977 when the UNP victory was marked by a string of unprovoked attacks in which more than 100 Tamils were killed. The defeat of the UNP in 1994 was accompanied by a temporary lessening of the rising tide of electoral violence, but recent elections have seen a return to the peaks of the late 1970s and early 1980s.

Nor is there anything in the subsequent political history of Sri Lanka to encourage such a comfortingly functional analysis of electoral ritual. Two months after the 1982 Presidential election, parliamentary elections were replaced by a referendum to extend the life of the existing parliament for a further term without any need for elections. The government won a victory in the referendum by massive use of fraud and intimidation. This was the moment of Cyril's underpants, celebrated in the Introduction to this book. The same gangs of UNP supporters who had doctored that result were out again in the summer of 1983, this time leading the anti-Tamil riots which tipped the country's ethnic crisis over the brink and into civil war. By the time that elections were held again, in 1988 and 1989, the north of the country was occupied by troops from the Indian Peace-Keeping Force, while in the south thousands were killed in the conflict between the young rebels of the JVP and the government. These elections were desperate, muted affairs with many electors terrified of voting in defiance of a JVP-called boycott. When I finally returned to Tenna in 1991, soon after the brutal suppression of the JVP rebellion, people hurriedly assured me, 'We are not interested in politics now.'

The conventional wisdom on the violence of the late 1980s blames the general problem of youth unrest on the economy, and especially on the lingering mismatch between young people's educational levels and their employment prospects. This, it seems to me, can only be part of the story. The official enquiry into the causes of the uprising emphasized the role played by a certain style of politics: 'What was underscored during our deliberations was not politics as "the art of governance" but the abuses and excesses of politicization which give rise to strong perceptions of injustice, especially among the young' (Presidential Commission on Youth 1990: 1). In other words, what animated the young rebels was moral revulsion at both the ubiquity of politics – in access to jobs and other opportunities – and also at its style. But they themselves acted in recognizably the same spirit as I have described: UNP members, government officials, and members of the security forces were targeted as bad or evil and killed; JVP suspects were tortured and massacred in return. There is no necessary and inevitable progression from a style of politics in which children are taught to sing that our side is good and the other side is bad, to a situation two decades later in which piles of defaced corpses by the roadside are an everyday sight. But we need to see the possible connections.

What, though, of the translation of ideas and institutions? Is this a straightforward case that can be treated as one more example from the growing literature on supposedly 'alternative modernities'? As Charles

Taylor puts it the 'modern state' and the 'modern economy' will be different in India, Japan, and North America: 'What comes out depends partly on what went into the change' (Taylor 1995: xi–xii). Here, after all, is a set of institutional procedures – elections, parties, representation – and here is a place with its own history, culture, and sociology. That history, culture, and sociology will necessarily shape the institutions into their local variants – democracy Lankan-style. I am less convinced by this argument now, for two reasons. One is the obvious one that, although this situation has its small peculiarities, it still looks a lot like 'politics' in a lot of other places. The Sri Lankan paradox of a combination of very high levels of political participation with very low expectations of the actions of politicians recurs across the subcontinent. To return to the earlier example from a village in West Bengal, 'Politics . . . represented a continuous social disturbance that caused unease, brought disharmony to society, and ruined its elaborate design and calm stability' (Ruud 2001: 116). Or Adams' informant in Nepal, also quoted in chapter one: 'So school is a very pure organization. Medicine should be the same. If politics is played here, it is going to spoil the school' (Adams 1998: 194–5). There are, at the least, family resemblances in the different readings of what politics is and what it is for across the subcontinent.

The second reason for my caution about a straightforwardly historical-cultural interpretation of the oddities of Sri Lankan politics is the way in which it conceives the relationship between institutions and interpretations. In this view, institutions like representative democracy are relatively inert, whereas interpretation is labile. But the institutions of representative democracy are not inert: they have their own dynamics, and the processes they set in train work through other areas of life in many ways, not all of them entirely as expected. Here is an important point of connection with recent political theory. Chantal Mouffe (2000), in a set of essays heavily influenced by the arguments of Schmitt, rehearses a critique of recent liberal theories of democracy. Mouffe's targets are the bland consensus politics of Tony Blair's 'Third Way', but her aim is to reinvigorate democratic thinking through engagement with anti-liberal critics like Schmitt. Deliberative theories of democracy, like those of Rawls and Habermas, she argues, seek to ground themselves in the possibility of consensus, however hypothetical or deferred that consensus may be. In contrast, Mouffe emphasizes the agonistic core of democracy, the need for adversarial positions, and the ways in which the workings of power *constitute* the very identities around which political competition works.

These, I would suggest, are the paradoxes and creative tensions which the villagers were trying to make sense of in their apprehension of the working of local politics. The rich and self-conscious local understanding of 'politics' as a temporary collective malaise represents an attempt to bound off, and thus make safe, the disturbing workings of something like Mouffe's 'agonistic pluralism'. The recourse to violence, especially in the years of terror in the late 1980s, reminds us how difficult this work of bounding really is (as well as why it such an attractive ideal). The identities – UNP and SLFP – around which village divisions mobilized had no coherent existence outside the domain of representative politics (although they omnivorously subsumed other identities with other histories – caste, religion, ethnicity). The roots of ethnic enmity and the coalescence of 'Tamil' and 'Sinhala' as opposed solidarities can be plausibly traced to the pattern of electoral politics in the first decade of mass democracy (the 1930s in Sri Lanka). These are not free-standing and self-evident divisions which somehow the political process has failed to 'manage': they are in many ways products of that very process.

If politics merely produced antagonisms that would be interesting, but hardly news to anyone who had followed an electoral campaign, anywhere in the world, ever (with the exception of some of the curious staged elections under state socialism). But the carnivalesque space of the political is a space of possibility and licence: licence to argue, and licence to joke, and licence to experiment with challenges to the order of things. It is, for this reason, also a space of danger, anxiety, and concern. In the 1930s the village I have described was a place where low-caste people could be beaten for walking too close to a high-caste person, and where the local landlords cultivated an aura of aristocratic detachment from the sordid lives of their tenants: they were greeted with gestures of worship, and addressed with elaborate honorifics and a language of utmost respect. In the very first elections, the tenants had the undoubted pleasure of watching leading members of those same aristocratic families exchange public insults of the coarsest sort, and enduring the very public humiliation of electoral defeat. Here is some of that corrosive power that Khilnani described in the quotation with which I opened this chapter.

There are many other things that happen in the space of the political, including not a little humour, fantasy, and entertainment. But two of the most important facets of what happens are the subjects of the next two chapters. In the space of the political, people have the opportunity to make some sense of that elusive presence, the state, not least as a source of social hope and social disappointment: that is the focus of the next chapter. Always in the background, to the experience of the state and to the perfomance of the political, is the possibility of violence, and violence is the subject of chapter six.

FIVE

States and Persons

In the early 1980s, separatist pressure in the prosperous agricultural heart-lands of the Punjab seemed briefly to threaten the survival of the Indian nation-state. Sikh followers of a charismatic leader, Sant Jarnail Bhin-dranwale, engaged in local skirmishes with Indian police and soldiers in pursuit of their campaign for an autonomous state of Khalistan. When Bhindranwale and his supporters took refuge in the holiest Sikh shrine, the Golden Temple in Amritsar, Indira Gandhi authorized the use of heavy force to dislodge them. Bhindranwale and many of his support-ers were killed in intense fighting, in which parts of the temple complex were also badly damaged. A few months later, Mrs Gandhi was assassi-nated by her two Sikh bodyguards, provoking waves of attacks on Sikhs in cities across North India, most of them organized by local Congress Party leaders. There followed a decade of escalating violence, in the Punjab and beyond, before the situation gradually calmed in the second half of the 1990s. As with the parallel case of northern Sri Lanka, many of the most dedicated supporters of Khalistan came from the extensive Sikh diaspora, especially in Britain, Canada, and the United States.

A few years ago, the American anthropologist Cynthia Keppley Mah-mood published an interesting book, based on her conversations with Sikh militants committed to the Khalistan movement. Much of the book is concerned to report, in as authentic a manner as possible, the self-descriptions, personal histories, and political vision of a group of people often labelled as 'terrorists', and subject to villification in both popular and academic media. Early on, though, the author records a moment of dissonance in the conversation, when one of her informants briefly discusses an obvious lacuna in his account of the movement for Khalistan. Mahmood's interlocutor suggests that 'the name of Khalistan came into existence' as late as 1983, only a year before Operation Blue Star, the Indian Army assault on the Golden Temple in Amritsar. And Bhindranwale himself, he says, 'did not so much have a "plan of action". Rather he was helping Khalistan emerge, letting the nation emerge, helping people become themselves as Sikhs' (Mahmood 1996: 66–7). Finally, he admits

I am just a reader of scriptures, I am not a politician. But it seems to me that it is a problem that there is no concrete plan for Khalistan, like a constitution or something, to show people what we are really fighting for. What we are fighting *against*, that is clear, but what are we fighting *for*? (Mahmood 1996: 71)

Mahmood tries to press the point, reminding the man of the need to look beyond the immediacy of the struggle, but the man drops the subject as their conversation is interrupted by the arrival of another, senior, activist. In her reflective conclusion to the book, Mahmood returns to this moment, and the problems 'for some' of a movement defined in a series of negatives, but vague on positives (Mahmood 1996: 260).

The question, though, is a good one. Confronted with the testimony in the rest of Mahmood's book – stories of torture by the Indian security forces, running weapons to the militants, bombs in a Hindu marketplace, and the calm murder of those identified as informants – it is hard not to ask, what is all this pain and suffering *for*? What animates and motivates these young people to court death in pursuit of a nebulous prospect, a state of their own, apparently imagined in the haziest of ways?

It is, as this opening example makes clear, no easy matter to think about the state in South Asia, or Africa or Latin America, and it is if anything harder in Sri Lanka. Since 1970, thousands of young people there have joined radical groups which have sought to challenge the state head-on, and capture state power by force. The first such manifestation was the 1971 Insurrection, a brief and quixotic rising by young people in the Sinhala-dominated south, many of them apparently radicalized in the election of 1970, and disappointed by the performance of the left-wing government they had helped elect. The state crushed their rising with some brutality and set the pattern for what was to follow. A few years later, the first militant attacks took place in Jaffna and, by the mid-1980s, the main Tamil insurgent group, the LTTE had grown into something more like a guerrilla army, capable of defeating the government's regular forces in open combat, and controlling large areas of the Tamil-speaking parts of the island. Finally, in 1987, after an abortive Indian-imposed peace initiative, the group responsible for the 1971 Insurrection, the JVP or People's Liberation Front, returned to violent conflict with the state. In the following years an unknown number were killed or disappeared, probably at least 50,000 and possibly many more (Chandraprema 1991; Moore 1993). For young people, joining groups like the LTTE and the JVP has involved a thorough-going self-transformation. This self-transformation is focused on the evils of the state-that-is and the transcendent potential of the imagined state-to-be. For example, consider this exchange between a young female cadre of the LTTE and the anthropologist Margaret Trawick in Eastern Province in 1996:

Have you noticed any changes in your mind or heart since joining the movement?

If I were at home, I could not do all these things. I have become even more ready to die. I see the suffering of the people and I have no fear about fighting and dying for them. Even if I die today, I will be satisfied. When people in the movement die, it is a useful death. If I died in the house, there would be nothing remarkable about that.

And later in the same interview

What will Tamil Eelam be like?

(laughs) The people will be happy. We must see that the people are happy, make them happy.

What kind of life do you desire for yourself?

I want the life of a fighter. That is the kind of life I like. I don't want an ordinary life.

The LTTE fighter continues with her explanation for her own rejection of marriage and domesticity and a lyrical account of her own impending death in the struggle: 'we are happy at the thought of our death in battle, because then we become part of history' (Trawick 1999: 154).

Let me draw out some of the implications of this extraordinary conversation. Here we have a movement dedicated to the construction of the new world of Tamil Ealam and the destruction of the illegitimate state of Sri Lanka, a movement which has done this by the most comprehensive remaking of its members as new people of the new nation. But the new state itself, like the imagined state of Khalistan far away in the north-west of the subcontinent, is dreamt of in the most sketchy way, while the real lyricism is focused on the imagining of death, the sweetness of the hero's death in particular. This invites an obvious question: Why is it 'the state' that should so powerfully shape the political and moral imagination of these young people – not least, if we bear in mind the apparent failures of the same state to address their current social and material predicament.

In this and the next chapter I want to address the question of the post-colonial state, with the specific issue of what we might expect an anthropology of the state to look like, and what we might expect it to contribute to our theoretical understanding of the postcolonial state. These opening examples highlight an important disjunction, which recurs through the argument that follows: this is the disjunction between the state as a complex of institutions and procedures, the 'state system' or 'apparatus' in Philip Abrams' (1988 [1977]) formulation, and the state as a vehicle for the political imagination, the so-called 'state idea'. What is it that makes the state as symbolic locus so 'good to think', yet makes the state as socio-political entity so hard to get hold of?

Biographies of State and Person

One place to start is with some thoughts from the Sri Lankan political theorist and activist, Jayadeva Uyangoda. In an essay published in the late 1990s, he drew attention to the intertwined biographies of his generation (he was born in 1950, three years after Independence) and the fledgling nation-state of Sri Lanka. He starts with a pivotal memory, the tales of ethnic violence that reached his village in the south in 1958, 'bringing', as he puts it, 'an entirely new level of political knowledge to that predominantly peasant society' (Uyangoda 1997: 171). Uyangoda's piece is not a complete autobiography, but the central idea of the intertwined biographies of state and generation is an enticing one, reminding us of two things. First, how the life of someone like Uyangoda, a student leader at the time of the 1971 Insurrection, and a leading peace campaigner through the years of civil war in the 1980s and 1990s, has been bent and shaped by the postcolonial history of the Sri Lankan state. But secondly, how both state and person are not stable figures, but protean entities, subject to growth, change and, he suggests, death too. The figure of the intertwined biography of person and nation is, of course, the very stuff of nationalist imaginings: either in the form 'We must make new men and women for the new nation'; or, more individualistically, 'I must remake myself as a preliminary to the remaking of the nation.' (The autobiography is, after all, *the* privileged site of nationalist reflection.) Forty years ago, Louis Dumont, drawing on his reading of Mauss, pointed out the formal symmetry between the idea of the nation and the idea of the individual: 'The nation is the political group conceived as a collection of individuals and, at the same time, in relation to other nations, the political individual' (Dumont 1980: 317). Little wonder, then, that the request 'tell me about your nation' – whether the nation in question is Khalistan, Eelam or, I suspect, 'India' or 'England' – produces embarrassed mumbling of the sort we might expect if we routinely asked our interlocutors, 'tell me about your person'.

Reviewing the academic literature on the decay of the nation-state in Sri Lanka, Uyangoda points to the centrality of anthropology as the discipline that has most succeeded in coming to terms with the political calamity. But the main lacuna that follows from that is 'the absence of a political theory concerning the nation-state and its consequences' (Uyangoda 1997: 169). Anthropologists have to start, then, with the apparently absurd questions: What *do* we mean by the state? Why is it so hard to make sense of, either empirically or theoretically? Is this simply a matter of scale: states are big, translocal institutions, anthropologists are miniaturists, bound to the familiar limits of their village or neighbourhood? Or is there something about the concept itself – at once necessary *and* incoherent – which makes it so good for dreaming but even more resistant to analysis?

Uyangoda's idea of a parallel biography of person and state suggests we might usefully borrow insights from recent anthropological writing on the self for insight into our understanding of the state. Debbora Battaglia, for example, describes selfhood as 'a chronically unstable productivity brought situationally – not invariably – to some form of imaginary order, to some purpose, as realized in the course of culturally patterned interactions' (Battaglia 1995: 2). What is said of the self could as easily be said of 'the state', a similarly unstable entity, and a similarly productive one, for which the appearance of order or unity is never more than situational and ephemeral. Battaglia's methodological suggestion is to look at the ways in which different models of selfhood are invoked, what she calls in the title of her book 'rhetorics of self-making', and to ask what *use* can be made of this or that different version of a self (Battaglia 1995: 3). So too with a state – under what circumstances might people bring forth an image of the state as a unitary agent, marked by certain traits, or the focus of particular desires? Equally, under what circumstances are the different material encounters with the state – the trip to school, the sight of a policeman driving by, the pursuit of a dispute through the courts – simply thought of as disparate encounters, particulars in the flow of life, rather than connected moments in our relationship with a single translocal personality. To borrow Battaglia's phrase, what might we learn from an ethnographic mapping of rhetorics of state-making, when language is pressed into the service of the state-as-unitary-presence, and from mappings of the rhetoric of state-unmaking, when language and practice seem to be focused on the task of obfuscating the separateness and unity of the state.

Idea and Apparatus

So far in this book, the main theoretical proposition about the state has been Ranajit Guha's assertion that the colonial state represented 'an *absolute externality . . . structured like a despotism*, with no mediating depths, no space provided for a transaction between the will of the rulers and that of the ruled' (Guha 1989: 274), and his strong implication that the postcolonial state retains many of these characteristics. A less clearly articulated version of this position runs through a huge amount of recent anthropology, in which the state can only be conceived as external, as a force to be resisted, with more or less heroism, by the plucky subjects of our field research. This is unconvincing, not least because it is based on misplaced confidence that, *a priori*, we 'know' what the state 'is' and what it 'does'. But it also fails to account for the moral investment that many people make in the idea of being owners, or at least members, of a state of their own.

In fact, one of the most common theoretical moves, which unites the unlikeliest of intellectual bedfellows – Michael Taussig *and* Radcliffe-Brown, francophile poststructuralists *and* crewcut 1950s political scientists – is to deny that there is such a 'thing' as the state at all. In anthropology the best-known version of this can be found in Radcliffe-Brown's

Preface to that landmark volume of British colonial anthropology, *African Political Systems*:

In writings on political institutions there is a good deal of discussion about the nature and origin of the State, which is usually represented as being an entity over and above the human individuals who make up a society, having as one of its attributes something called 'sovereignty', and sometimes spoken of as having a will (law often being defined as the will of the State) or as issuing commands. The State in this sense does not exist in the phenomenal world; it is a fiction of the philosophers. What does exist is an organization, i.e. a collection of individual human beings connected to a complex set of relations . . . There is no such thing as the power of the State; there are only, in reality, powers of individuals – kings, prime ministers, magistrates, policemen, party bosses and voters. (Radcliffe-Brown 1940: xxiii)

The British *marxisant* sociologist Philip Abrams, writing in the late 1970s, quoted Radcliffe-Brown in support of an argument (to which I will return) which started with the suggestion that 'the problem of the state may be in an important sense a fantasy', or 'a spurious object of sociological concern' (Abrams 1988 [1977]: 63). In fact, as Timothy Mitchell (1991) makes clear in a justifiably celebrated piece, there is nothing especially challenging in identifying problems in empirically separating out 'the state' from 'society': in the 1950s, political scientists favoured constructions like 'the political system' in order to side-step just those difficulties. Nor is there anything particularly new in locating the state in the domain of symbols: David Easton had made just such a claim in the early 1950s and Peter Nettl had defined the state as 'essentially a socio-cultural phenomenon' or a 'cultural disposition' in the 1960s (Mitchell 1991: 81).

Mitchell's own argument hinges on the elusive boundary between state and society, which on the one hand 'never marks a real exterior', but on the other hand 'is itself a mechanism that generates resources of power', by, for example, strategically excluding certain topics and activities from the explicit responsibility of the state (Mitchell 1991: 90). Following Foucault,

Mitchell argues that what we call the state is less important than the per-vasive modes of discipline, regulation, and surveillance that characterize modern forms of power. The state itself – and specifically the illusion of a separate, bounded entity standing apart from society – can be seen as an *effect* of these modern disciplinary practices. The illusion is now what holds it all together:

> The state should be addressed as an effect of spatial organization, tempo-ral arrangement, functional specification, and supervision and surveillance, which create the appearance of a world fundamentally divided into state and society. The essence of modern politics is not policies formed on one side of this division being applied to or shaped by the other, but the producing and reproducing of this line of difference. (Mitchell 1991: 95).

These different arguments coalesce around a number of points. While it is apparently useful to talk casually about 'the state' as a unitary entity, and even, in some cases, to attribute intentionality and personality to it, empirically it is much harder to isolate and define a unitary 'thing', standing apart from and above the social. And, although this is not an issue for the particular writers discussed so far, there is something especially absurd in treating all variants of the postcolonial state, from the crumbling polities of central Africa to the antiseptic authoritarianism of Singapore, as essentially the same. Nevertheless, we live in a world where we routinely encounter the boundaries of the state: on international frontiers, but also stepping into an office or a police station, or responding to a tax demand. 'We' are apparently on one side, and 'it' is on the other. The point is, though, that this distinction is not simply given in the order of things, nor is it self-evident, rather it has to be endlessly made and remade. For Mitchell, this work of boundary-making is part of a wider pattern of modern disciplinary power, and the 'state-effect' is but one particular instance of a more general production of 'abstraction' in which the state, like 'the economy', appears as 'a nonmaterial totality that seems to exist apart from the material world of society' (Mitchell 1991: 91).

Abrams' article pushes this idea of the state, as something abstracted from material circumstances, in an especially interesting direction. He makes a distinction between the 'state-system' – 'a palpable nexus of practice and institutional structure centred in government and more or less extensive, unified and dominant in any given society' (Abrams 1988 [1977]: 82) – and the 'state-idea' as an 'ideological power':

> My suggestion, then, is that we should recognize that cogency of the *idea* of the state as an ideological power and treat that as a compelling object of analysis. But the very reasons that require us to do that also require us not to *believe* in the idea of the state, not to concede, even as an abstract formal-object, the existence of the state. (Abrams 1988 [1977]: 79–80)

If Abrams has provided us with a useful organizing motif for this chapter, in the form of a provisional distinction between 'system' and 'idea', the 'palpable' and the 'ideological', he has also, perhaps less helpfully, provided an anthropologically dangerous injunction: rather like a hardcore freethinker calling on God to prove himself with a bolt of lightning, he *requires* us not to admit 'the existence of the state' – even for a moment.

The injunction is perilous for anthropologists because, like an equivalent command to students of religion, it drives an intellectual wedge between the ethnographer and any informant who dares to subscribe to the delusion. The result is some happy sport for enthusiastic practitioners of the hermeneutics of suspicion. From the anthropology of religion, we know that boundaries are the place of taboo, and that taboo invites transgression, which is at once powerful and dangerous. Desire and disgust, the sacred and the erotic, life and death: we return once more to the notion of ambivalence:

> My concern lies with this endless flight in modern times back and forth from the hard-edged thing to its ephemeral ghost and back again, which, in what must surely seem a wild gesture, I see as a spin-off of what I plan to call *State fetishism* . . . It is to the peculiar sacred and erotic attraction, even thraldom,

combined with disgust, which the State holds for its subjects that I wish to draw attention in my drawing the figure of State fetishism, and here we would do well to recall that for Nietzsche, good and evil, intertwined in the double helix of attraction and repulsion, are so much aesthetic-moralistic renderings of the social structure of might. (Taussig 1992: 111)

Taussig's high-octane prose can sustain itself for the length of a short essay, and his central idea, of the non-rational core of danger, excess and fantasy at the heart of the 'state-idea', is an important one. But the development of this idea, in *The Magic of the State* (Taussig 1997), a book which deliberately presents itself as an ethnography of a 'fictive nation-state', is less engaging. The organizing conceit of writing a magical realist ethnography misses the political point spectacularly. In the end, who cares about a fictional ethnography of a fictional state? Whatever it is that stirs the young militants I quoted at the start of this chapter, it is something more substantial, more serious, and, to challenge this chapter's animating distinction between idea and system, for them more *real* than anything we might read in Taussig's arch imitation of Marquez and Rushdie. In the end, there is a difference, as Talal Asad eloquently reminds us, between treating 'the state' as an abstraction, and treating it as an illusion (Asad 2004: 282).

Blurred Boundaries

I will return to ambivalence, and the imaginative properties of the 'state idea', at the end of the next chapter. First, though, let me provide some more empirical documentation for the theoretical case made in the last section. Is the state self-evidently separated from society? If not, how are boundaries asserted and what happens when they are transgressed?

In a celebrated essay, Akhil Gupta describes the work of a minor official, a *patwari* or land registrar in western Uttar Pradesh. The man is called Sharmaji, and the following is taken from Gupta's description of his 'office, one room open to the street in an unmarked building in the old part of town':

Two of the side walls of the office were lined with benches; facing the entrance toward the inner part of the room was a raised platform, barely big enough for three people. It was here that Sharmaji sat and held court, and it was here that he kept the land registers for the villages that he administered. All those who had business to conduct came to this 'office'. At any given time there were usually two or three different groups, interested in different transactions, assembled in the tiny room. Sharmaji conversed with all of them at the same time, often switching from one addressee to another in the middle of a single sentence. Everyone present joined in the discussion of matters pertaining to others. Sharmaji often punctuated his statements by turning to the others and rhetorically asking, 'Have I said anything wrong?' or, 'Is what I have said true or not?' (Gupta 1995: 379)

Where, we might ask, is 'the state' in this particular space? Both the style of Sharwaji's activity, and its locus, dissolve any pretence to detached bureaucratic rationality in his work, and with this goes any ability to detect where 'the state' ends and other forms of sociality begin. That, of course, is the point. It follows that the distinction between 'state' and 'civil society', born as it is of a particular, and peculiarly Western, historical experience is 'descriptively inadequate' to the 'lived realities' of postcolonial South Asia (Gupta 1995: 384).

Gupta's article takes on a number of issues at once – the problematic relationship between notions of 'locality' and translocal institutions like the postcolonial Indian state, the role of discourses of 'corruption' in *constructing* a representation of something we might call 'the state', and the methodological challenge posed for anthropology in studying such a large and diffuse entity, a challenge Gupta meets by combining ethnographic data with material from mass media sources like newspapers and television. What emerges from the rich idiom of corruption in smalltown North India is extremely interesting. On the one hand, there is the sheer ubiquity of what we might call 'corruption' in people's everyday experiences of the local state: the need for connections and backhanders in order to gain access to crucial resources like loans and housing. Secondly, there is the practical difficulty of mastering what Gupta calls the performative aspects of corruption: knowing what is an appropriate offering, knowing who it should be offered to, knowing how to offer it. Thirdly, and this I feel deserves more comment than Gupta provides, there is the complex sociology of corruption. In particular, corruption involves far more than a simple dyadic instrumental relation: A gives to B in return for B's assistance in gaining access to state resources. One drama that unfolds in Sharmaji's office involves two young men, acting together (but probably representing a broader group in the village from which they come), Sharmaji and his aides, and a complex etiquette of approach which eventually defeats the uncouth supplicants. Later examples include a poor villager whose potential gains from a government housing programme are thwarted by the village headman and the village development worker until the villager successfully draws the attention of a much higher authority, the District Magistrate, to the problem. The most spectacular cases involved frustrated farmers who take direct collective action against corrupt local officials whose reluctance to part with crucial transformers leaves the farmers' wells out of action. As well as further blurring the state–society boundary, these final examples illustrate the complexity of people's potential 'constructions' of the local state. Crucially, the discourse of corruption is not a simple discourse of amoral instrumentalism; it is also potentially a discourse of moral evaluation, and this in turn can create space for new expressions of collective agency, as exemplified by the protests of the angry farmers.

This is from an interview with a prosperous low-caste man called Ram Singh some months before the national elections in December 1989: 'The public is singing the praises of Rajiv. He is paying really close attention to the needs of poor people . . . Rajiv has been traveling extensively in the rural areas and personally finding out the problems faced by the poor. For this reason, I will definitely support the Congress (I)' (Gupta 1995: 390). Gupta successfully unpacks much of what is going on in this peroration on the virtues of Rajiv's Congress. First of all, and perhaps most obviously, this is a man who watches a lot of television. He watches a lot of television because his family is one of a handful in the village who own a set, and this because of their relative prosperity which owes not a little to Congress support of education and employment for Scheduled Castes in the area in the past. Television gives him a point of orientation in his conversations, as well, it seems, as a distinctive language for commenting on public events ('Rajiv has been traveling extensively in the rural areas'). Gupta comments on Ram Singh's sophisticated ability to differentiate the government from the bureaucracy, and his 'layered' sense of the state. Ram Singh's evaluation of Rajiv's progress invokes a crucial category – 'the public' who, he says, are singing Rajiv's praises. In talking of 'the public', Ram Singh is using that category for himself and implicitly placing himself firmly within it. In other words, it is not simply, as Gupta argues, that 'The government . . . is being constructed here in the imagination and everyday practices of ordinary people' (Gupta 1995: 390). It is also that, in reflecting on 'the government', people may acquire a new sense of themselves as belonging to that extraordinary category, 'the ordinary people'. This, I would suggest, represents a small but real increase in the vocabulary of social and political possibility, and this is the point which, I shall argue at the end of the next chapter, links Gupta's North Indian farmers and petty officials to the Khalistan activists and the militants of the LTTE with whom I started.

Rough Governmentality

One of the most important intellectual sources for recent critical analysis of the postcolonial state is, of course, the work of Michel Foucault. Yet Foucault, in one of his most cited lectures, 'On Governmentality', was concerned to downplay the importance of 'the state' as an intellectual or political problem:

But the state, no more probably today than at any other time in its history, does not have this unity, this individuality, this rigorous functionality, nor, to speak frankly, this importance; maybe, after all, the state is no more than a composite reality and a mythicized abstraction, whose importance is a lot more limited than many of us think. Maybe what is really important for our modernity – that is, for our present – is not so much the *étatisation* of society, as the 'governmentalization' of the state. (Foucault 1991a: 103)

By 'governmentalization' Foucault is referring to a nexus of institutions, of objects, and of disciplines – especially 'population' and 'economy' as objects of knowledge and zones for systematic intervention – that took hold in Western European society at some point in the eighteenth century. The shift from sovereignty to governmentality, as sketched in the lecture, is clearly thought of as singular and apparently irreversible.

More generally, Foucault's concerns are strikingly and deliberately indifferent to the kinds of evidence that anthropologists have most valued. His characteristic method is not to attempt to recover the lived world of, say, the nineteenth-century prison, but rather to elucidate the rationality embedded in particular programmes of reform, and to trace some of the effects of that rationality as it meets, complements, reinforces, sometimes clashes with, other programmes. Perhaps the most celebrated example is his discussion in *Discipline and Punish* (Foucault 1977: 200–9) of Jeremy Bentham's plan for a model prison based on surveillance and self-surveillance, the so-called Panopticon – a blueprint for an institution that was never actualy constructed. 'If I had wanted to describe "real life" in the prisons', as Foucault once observed, 'I wouldn't indeed have gone to Bentham' (Foucault 1991b: 81). Foucault is concerned to show how the ideal schemas found in a source like Bentham's plan for the Panopticon may nevertheless have 'real' effects: 'they crystallize into institutions, they inform individual behaviour, they act as grids for the perception and evaluation of things' (Foucault 1991b: 81). But none of this is to be confused with what he calls the 'admirable' project of 'grasping a "whole society" in its "living reality"' (Foucault 1991b: 82).

This is where we might hope for a really creative engagement with Foucault's work: the guerrilla theorist, forever concerned to unsettle the received wisdom, meets the practitioners of the improvisatory science, always alert to the unexpected. Yet one part of the routinization of Foucault's work in recent anthropology has been a retreat to the textual, to the formulaic reading 'against the grain', of this or that colonial or administrative document, readings which usually demonstrate the disciplinary rationale behind official discourse and the apparently inevitable making of modern bodies and modern subjects. If this starts to look too much like modernization theory retold in a Nietszchean key, then there is always the trope of resistance, the resort to some cultural space *beyond* the disciplinary grid of the modern state. The world of much anthropology in the Foucaultian mould is a very predictable world, a feel-good dystopia, where external power meets local cultural resistance, and the last surviving remnant of Foucault's bracing capacity to shock is drowned in a sea of sentimentality.

There are, though, counter-examples. The most remarkable recent anthropological evidence on the relationship between state projects and their local reception is Emma Tarlo's brilliant work on memories of the 1970s Emergency in a Delhi slum colony with the incongruous name of Welcome (Tarlo 2000; Tarlo 2001; Tarlo 2003). Her study makes an important point about the evidence we use in talking about the state. But it also allows us to extend and develop the argument about the blurred boundary between state and society. It concerns the working of modern forms of power on the bodies of the poor, but rather than treating her evidence as one more example from the familiar script of biopower and resistance, Tarlo instead documents an emergent rationality which grew out of the collision between official plans, local politics, and the unruly capacity of the people concerned to respond in their own way to what had been planned for them.

In 1975 the Indian Supreme Court found the then Prime Minister Indira Gandhi guilty of electoral malpractice and barred her from public office for a period of six years. Instead of accepting the Court's judgement, Mrs Gandhi declared a State of Emergency and initiated a period of nineteen months of unprecedented authoritarian rule, with rigid press censorship and the arrest and detention of her political opponents. The Emergency is also remembered for the government's vigorous pursuit of policies of slum clearance and forced sterilization in urban North India. These were the special concern of Mrs Gandhi's favoured son, Sanjay. Although it was widely rumoured at the time that state officials had required poor slum-dwellers to undergo sterilization if they were to be rehoused in new colonies, this was strenuously denied by the government.

In the early 1990s, Tarlo stumbled across an extraordinary cache of evidence in the records room of a local office of the slum wing of the Delhi Development Authority. There, amongst the dead rats and pigeon-shit, she and an assistant went through over 3,000 individual housing files. Juxtaposed within them she found a tell-tale combination of allotment slips and other bureaucratic documents – letters, death certificates, and, in many of them, something called a Family Planning Centre Allotment Order. This explicitly linked what was officially supposed never to have happened – records of sterilization and allocation of housing entitlements. In an important article, Tarlo (2001) recreates the site of her discovery in telling detail, for the setting itself, the records room and its attendant official minders, is an important part of her analysis. As she worked through the files, workers from the slum office would stop by and chat, reminiscing with disarming candour about their activities in the mid-1970s.

Her fundamental discovery was of the systematic lack of fit between the colony as it was and the colony as it appeared in paper form in the record room. Officials would explain how a counter-intuitive assemblage of documentary evidence would be reconciled in real-life dealings. In the Emergency, though, this gap between the official and the unofficial became the zone of pressure. As Tarlo puts it:

[I]n the mid-1970s [the colony] was home to a number of people who were living in the loophole between official policies and officially recognized irregularities. During the emergency that loophole tightened. It became a noose which squeezed its victims into participation in family planning, by offering them a choice between getting sterilized, paying someone else to get sterilized, or losing their access to land altogether. (Tarlo 2001: 83)

But, as Tarlo's last sentence indicates, what happened was not a straightforward trade-off of land for sterilization. What was officially required to document a case of sterilization was not evidence on the body of the would-be colony dweller, but evidence on paper. For the purposes of housing allocation, it was immaterial who had been sterilized so long as *someone* had been sterilized. So a market sprang up in sterilization certificates, with go-betweens arranging sterilizations on behalf of housing applicants, who would pay a sum of money to arrange for someone else to go through the operation. (The bureaucrats, remember, were working to meet target figures for total sterilizations, so all that mattered was the aggregate number of operations.)

On the face of it, this is an especially chilling example of the workings of what Foucault called modern biopower, the regulation of everyday power through the regulation of modern bodies. But Tarlo is eager to resist too simple a reading along these lines. Instead she emphasizes collusion as well as coercion, as poor people, not themselves part of the state apparatus, took part, sometimes enthusiastically, in the informal economy of reproductive potential. This is another story which cannot be fitted into the Manichean divide between power and resistance. It is a story again about the porous boundary between state and subject, only this time, rather than citizens actively subverting the boundaries of the official, it is the state's reforming energies which overflow its boundaries and percolate through other relations. The situation of the Emergency, as Tarlo acknowledges, *was* unusual, although the kinds of strategies people used to deal with it recur in other dealings with power and the state. The energies of the informal economy are themselves prodigious. The lineaments of the sterilization campaign – who in the end did what to whom – reproduce other, longer-standing inequalities. The middle class successfully pass the burden of state policy down to the poor: some of the recipients successfully pass it on to others, a few find ways to profit in the new situation, a few are unambiguous losers. The local boss, whose letters from the 1970s crop up in the files, is still there, still controlling his four blocks of colony. 'What happened during the Emergency', Tarlo concludes, 'was an intensification of dynamics and relationships already in existence' (Tarlo 2000: 263).

Boundaries and Performances

So far, I have been exploring the boundary, apparently porous and illusory, between the state and its subjects. But there is another sense in which the state is thought to have boundaries: passing from one state to another we have to go though the liminal world of passports and officials and border-guards, of customs officers behind one-way mirrors and body searches. As Taussig (1992) reminds us in his essay on 'State Fetishism', the border, the port, is the place where the state's erotic quality is most apparent. But these borders, and their transgression, link to more mundane workings of the political. In 1993 most of the Muslim residents of Welcome (and some of the Hindus too) were officially told they were in fact Bangladeshi (Tarlo 2000: 261). Those who could find the right documentary evidence were subsequently redefined as Indians, but those who could not were removed from the electoral rolls. In Sri Lanka after Independence a whole category of the population, the so-called Indian Tamils, were politically disenfranchised, this time because they were deemed to be 'really' Indian rather than Ceylonese; from the 1960s many of them were removed to a country most had never seen (Spencer 2003).

The background to the Welcome case is rather different. The boundary between India and Bangladesh is long and, for the most part, poorly controlled. But, as Ranabir Samaddar (Samaddar 1999) makes clear, the widespread transgression of this border can be seen to be linked to a much wider network of politics and violence across North India. In the end, the states on either side of the border cannot hope to control the flow of population back and forth. Poor Bangladeshi migrants to the cities can provide client armies for local political bosses. The existence of the category 'illegal migrant' can, as in Welcome, be used to exclude sections of the urban poor from the political process. In a perverse way, Samaddar argues, those who transgress the border are *necessary* to the system as a whole:

Migrants and refugees always remain on the margins of the system – they are there to be ignored, to be eternally peripheralized. But they are required to define the system, to define the core and the periphery of the nations in South Asia. The 'illegal' migration makes possible a mode of political and economic management which exploits the difference between legal and the illegal; migrant labour, therefore, becomes one of the principal forms of the investment of national boundaries with power. (Samaddar 1999: 44)

In short, if they did not exist, the state would have to invent them. Without transgression, how can we tell what is normal?

Samaddar develops this point in some suggestive opening remarks in his monograph. The border, he says, is essential to the naturalization of statecraft. And, in a formulation which echoes some of Tarlo's reading of the colony records, 'Statecraft must, therefore, thrive on ambiguity' (Samaddar 1999: 21). Samaddar's own argument focuses on the political and imaginative economy of 'the illegal migrant' in South Asia, but we can take his central point and push it further. Rather than imagining the relationship between 'the state', its projects, and the world, as one of the gradual actualization of a blueprint, the making of the world in the image of a certain rationality, we could start from the central ambiguity of statecraft, its failure to produce a world in the terms it expects. In this formulation statecraft does not produce a world, or subjects, or spaces for social or political action: rather statecraft is better seen as performative, it attempts to enact a version of the world against a background of dissonance and transgression. The border is where the state performs its rites of order and control, even as the illegals walk across after the guards have gone to bed.

This version of statecraft can be developed in at least two different directions. In Tarlo's account of the workings of local bureaucrats, the world never corresponds to the version that is necessarily recorded on paper. The lack of fit leaves space for negotiation, fixing, a little room to breathe and a little space to improvise. But, when pressure is suddenly applied from above, this space of ambiguity becomes the point of pressure: because no one's papers can ever be truly in order, all can be made to obey the new dictates. On the other hand, the skills acquired by living in the gap behind ideal and actuality can themselves threaten the state and its projects. The leaders of those LTTE cadres with which I started this chapter come from villages and families which have for a century or more lived from crossing and recrossing the short stretch of sea which separates Sri Lanka from India, illegally moving people and goods. Mahmood's Khalistan militants tell tales of clandestine movement, smuggling weapons under the noses of the police and army. When the state applied pressure on dissent, those most adept at improvisation in the zone of ambiguity provide the backbone of the opposition. More starkly still, in those West African polities where the state has all but abandoned its bureaucratic project, we are confronted instead with a statecraft of pure performance, the politics of what Mbembe (1992) calls the *commandement*.

The key to this understanding of the workings of the state is a very old one and a very anthropological one: it is to pay attention to what people say they do (or what official documents say they should be doing), and also to what they actually do. And, noting the inevitable discrepancy between the two, it is to compose an understanding of what happens in which this discrepancy is not an accident or an embarrassment, but is in fact central to what is happening. It involves a combination of wide-eyed empiricism – looking at what is actually there – and the most critical and suspicious of interpretations.

SIX

∾

The State and Violence

If you are the victim of a crime, there is a proper sequence of events to follow. If, for example, you discover a thief has made off with the money you had hidden away in your house, you go to the police, give them 1,000 rupees and tell them who you think did it. The police will arrest this person, take them to the police station, and beat them up. At this point, friends and relatives of the arrested person will usually bring a further 1,000 rupees to the police, who will set the first suspect free, but come and arrest you, take you to the police station and beat you up. At this point, you need to find another 1,000 rupees. Few crimes are solved, and even fewer produce convictions before the courts, while even the emotional satisfaction of revenge is purely temporary. All that really happens is the police get richer. Or, in the fastidious phrasing of a senior British diplomat I once met in Colombo, the problem for the police in a country like Sri Lanka, is that they 'lack forensic capacity'.[1]

I thought of this story (first told to me in Sri Lanka in the early 1980s) in September 1997, when I attended a training course in human rights and gender awareness for senior police officers in Sri Lanka. I was interested in policing as an aspect of the 'everyday state'. An old friend had been commissioned to co-ordinate this course as part of a general push

---

[1] For vivid examples of the consequences of this 'lack' see the report on everyday policing by the Hong Kong-based Asian Human Rights Commission (2004).

to clean up the country's human rights act. Before I knew it, I was lighting the ceremonial oil-lamp to inaugurate the first session. In a spirit of interactive pedagogy, my friend asked each policeman to introduce himself to the other participants, and explain why he had signed up for the course. The first policeman spoke rather sheepishly. 'My name is . . . , I am Officer in Charge at . . . I joined the police in 1984 and I came on this course because I have five fundamental rights cases outstanding against me.' The second was much the same, a different name, a different station, this time four rights cases. And so it went on as we progressed round the room. Every officer there was under investigation for violation of someone's human rights. Later, I asked a senior policeman, who stopped by to check on proceedings, about this. 'Well', he explained, 'these people are used to beating people up if they suspect them of something, and in the 1980s if the politicians told them to do something like this, they had to do it. Now the politicians tell them they mustn't beat people up after all, it's a matter of human rights. They are here because they are confused.'

This kind of story takes us back, albeit in unexpected ways, to Weber's classic definition of the state as a putative monopolist of legitimate force (a definition which has mysteriously lost its capacity to disturb) (Weber 1978: 54). Somewhere in the juxtaposition between the cynicism of the policemen I met in Colombo, and the unfocused idealism of the young militants quoted at the start of the previous chapter, we may, I believe, begin to find the missing link between the state as an institutional apparatus and the state as a space for the political imagination. The link is provided by the semiotic capacities of violence, and its place in the configuration of sovereignty in the postcolonial world. I will try to work through this juxtaposition in the final part of this chapter, but first I want to review anthropology's contribution to understandings of the relationship between the state, the political, and collective violence in South Asia. I will do this through an examination of anthropological responses to two 'critical events' (Das 1995b) – the July 1983 anti-Tamil violence in Sri Lanka, and the anti-Sikh violence in Delhi the following year. Although conventional representations of these events emphasize their 'extraordinary' quality, I want to argue that this is a mystification which lifts them out of the flow of normal time, and bounds them off from the space of the everyday. We need, I suggest, to interpret events like these as occurring in what I call 'political time' and as located in 'political space'. In other words, collective violence should not be treated as a departure from the flow of the political, but rather should be analysed as a heightened and intensified continuation of normal politics.

The Anthropology of the 1983 Violence

The events of July 1983 had a transforming effect on the modern history of Sri Lanka; and in a more minor key, they were instrumental in transforming the research agenda of Sri Lankan anthropology. In terms of sheer nastiness, these events have been thoroughly eclipsed by the horrors of the late 1980s and after, but 1983 has remained the key date in academic and political argument alike. Around 3,000 people are thought to have died in the July violence in 1983, whereas estimates for the death toll in the 1987–90 JVP rising start at 40,000 and go up from there, while figures for deaths in the two decades of civil war in the north and east of the island hover between 60,000 and 100,000. But all these later horrors can be quite easily traced back to what happened in that week in 1983, and 1983 remains the iconic year in both academic and popular representations of Sri Lanka's troubles.

In anthropology before 1983, Sri Lankan ethnographies mostly fell into two types: those concerned with issues of kinship, property, and livelihood, working in the tradition founded by Edmund Leach in the early 1960s, and those concerned with religion, ritual, and social change, which often took their point of departure from one of the virtuoso essays on Buddhism and society published by Gananath Obeyesekere in the same decade.[2] After 1983, anthropologists turned their attention to nationalism and political violence, to the extent that, by the mid-1990s, anthropology had established itself as the dominant academic discipline concerned with the interpretation of Sri Lanka's political crisis (Uyangoda 1997). This in turn exposed anthropologists and their work to criticism from ultra-nationalist polemicists. The most spectacular example occurred in the early 1990s when Stanley Tambiah's *Buddhism Betrayed?* (1992) – a book critical of certain styles of political Buddhism, written by a scholar of Tamil origins – was banned by the Colombo government following a vitriolic campaign in the Sri Lankan media. After this, anthropology was increasingly identified by local hard-liners as an inherently 'anti-national' intellectual exercise. (This is the background to the controversy with which I closed chapter three.)

The conventional story of the July 1983 violence runs something like this. On Saturday, 23 July members of the LTTE ambushed a group of soldiers in the Jaffna peninsula, killing thirteen of them (by far the highest death-toll sustained by the security forces at that early stage in the conflict). On 24 July, the bodies were brought to Colombo for burial at the main cemetery. A crowd gathered and went on to attack Tamil property in the area. The next day the attacks spread to Tamil property across Colombo, and on the 26th the government declared a curfew across the country. In the days that followed, Tamil-owned targets in towns outside Colombo were attacked. As well as attacks on property, there were intermittent but sometimes hideous attacks on people too: cars and their occupants were set alight, families burned alive in their houses. In Colombo's main prison, fifty-two Tamil prisoners, many of them separatist activists, were ritually humiliated and murdered by their fellow

---

[2] Examples of the 'materialist' tradition would include Leach (1961), Obeyesekere (1967), Yalman (1967), Brow (1978), Alexander (1995), and Stirrat (1988). The influence of Obeyesekere's analyses of Buddhism and society permeates works like Gombrich (1971), Seneviratne (1976), Obeyesekere (1981), Kapferer (1983), Gombrich and Obeyesekere (1988), Stirrat (1992), and Brow (1996).

prisoners. On Friday the 29th, Colombo was swept by rumours of an LTTE attack in the heart of the city: workers fled their city-centre offices, while police and soldiers exchanged shots, each convinced the other was the enemy from the north. At the time, the government announced a suspiciously precise death-toll of less than 400 for the week's violence, but other estimates varied between 1,000 and 3,000.[3]

As well as numerous articles and reviews, the 1983 violence framed the research that fed into two major anthropological monographs. Bruce Kapferer was in Colombo from 1984 to 1985, originally planning to research sorcery shrines, but, alert to the political pressures of the time, he used some of the year to draft his *Legends of People, Myths of State* (Kapferer 1988: xi–xv). Valentine Daniel arrived in Sri Lanka immediately after the 1983 violence, with an SSRC research grant to collect Tamil women's folk songs: his interviews with the survivors of this, and subsequent, violence make up the core of his *Charred Lullabies: Chapters in an Anthropography of Violence* (Daniel 1996).

Kapferer's book is a comparative study of nationalism and intolerance in Sri Lanka and Australia. Although it has had considerable success amongst anthropologists in general, it has been much more critically received by Sri Lanka specialists (Spencer 1989; Scott 1990; Woost 1994). The book is based on a strong contrast between two case-studies, Australian nationalism and Sinhala nationalism, a contrast which

---

[3] The 1983 violence has been the subject of a large, if uneven, literature. Manor (1984) collects a number of accounts written by academic authors, many of whom were in the island at the time of the violence; my own contribution to that collection was an account from the limited perspective of a village many miles from the centres of trouble (Spencer 1984). In the late 1980s I collated as much information as was then available in a critical response to Kapferer's (1988) monograph, which while obviously intended as an analysis of the 1983 violence, contained almost no first-hand evidence on the violence itself (Spencer 1990a). The 1983 violence provides a setting for some of the vignettes in Daniel's *Charred Lullabies* (Daniel 1996), and is a key case-study in two recent comparative books on collective violence by Tambiah (1996) and Horowitz (2001). No precise death-toll has ever been announced for the week's events. The most useful recent collation of evidence can be found in Hoole's *Sri Lanka: The Arrogance of Power* (2001).

Kapferer interprets in terms of Louis Dumont's (1980) dichotomy between the egalitarian and the hierarchical. The book also tackles an important but difficult question: how to allow space for the cultural particularity of specific nationalisms, while acknowledging the dangers of tautology because these are ideological projects explicitly concerned with assertions of cultural particularity. In order to wrestle his way out of the contradictions that follow, Kapferer posits a number of objects for analysis – 'ideology', 'culture', 'political culture', 'cosmology', 'cultural logic', and 'ontology' – as if the demons of essentialism could be held at bay by the smoke and mirrors of abstraction. An ontology, or cultural logic, to be discerned in nationalist cosmology and everyday practice alike, shapes the political culture, and as realized in ideology, and instantiated in particular historical circumstances, has the potential to sway the hearts of national subjects. In Sinhala nationalist cosmology, nation and state are one, and an attack upon the state is an attack upon the person. Difference, in the form of non-Buddhist minorities, can always be incorporated but at the cost of hierarchical subordination:

My suggestion is plain. The Sri Lankan Buddhist state and the Sinhalese people are obviously in dangerous and reciprocal conjunction. An attack on Sinhalese is an attack on the state, and an attack on the organs or apparatuses of the state is an attack on the person. There is every reason, given the ontology I have discussed, for Sinhalese to take very personally indeed any opposition to the state by persons who are ontologically foreign and threatening to the hierarchical and encompassing unity of the state. Here is a reason, extraordinary as it may seem, for the sudden, almost inexplicable, transformation of a normally peaceful people into violent and murderously rampaging mobs. (Kapferer 1988: 100–1)

Empirically, Kapferer's Sri Lankan argument is built upon two sources: his own ethnography of sorcery and exorcism practices, and his reading of the English translation of the Buddhist chronicle, the Mahavamsa. Although this part of the book is directly shaped by Kapferer's response to the 1983 events, it contains no detailed description of the violence itself, relying instead on some rather lurid generalizations: the riots 'were of a savagery unparalleled' in the history of the ethnic conflict, Sinhala gangs roamed around with lists of Tamil targets, 'systematically burning them and slaughtering their inhabitants'. 'The fury of the riots', the reader is told, 'was demonic' (Kapferer 1988: 29).

In contrast, *Charred Lullabies* (Daniel 1996) is one of the best and subtlest books to come out of the Sri Lankan crisis. Its opening chapters overlap with some of Kapferer's material in their exploration of the heavy burden brought by the past to our understanding of Sri Lanka's troubles. But little by little, the book becomes an exercise in witness and the possibilities and impossibilities of personal testimony. If there is a central motif in the book, it is of the torture survivor who denies that anyone else shared his experience, a lone figure against a background of horror:

Torture perverts all dialogic. For the victim's interlocutor is not that person's parent, friend, or child. The interlocutor is not even a mere stranger but rather the torturer, for whom a scream is not a sign of pain but an insignia of power. And even after the torture victim is set free, regardless of the readiness of friends and kinsfolk who remained free to extend love, understanding, and sympathy, the victim persists in denying that his individuated pain could be shared, contained as it is within the bounds of a private body that is reticent to express itself willingly through any signs in general and incapable of expressing itself in signs of language in particular. (Daniel 1996: 143)

But pain might find its expression in poetry or music, and Daniel's subsequent account of the gradual recovery of culture and the intersubjective offers a thin skein of hope in a situation of desperate hopelessness. Ultimately, Daniel uses his interviews with survivors of political violence to compose something rather unexpected: a postmodern meditation on what the experience of violence tells us about human nature. The book, which intellectually owes much to Heideggerian anti-humanism, concludes with a strong reassertion of a certain, rather specific, anthropological humanism.

Violence in Political Time

For all their differences, Daniel and Kapferer share one feature in the shape their analyses take, and that is a kind of separation of violence from the flow of what I am calling 'political time'. This is most apparent in Kapferer's invocation of the 'sudden, almost inexplicable, transformation of a normally peaceful people into violent and murderously rampaging mobs' (Kapferer 1988: 101). As a formulation, it focuses attention on sudden change, on contrast, rather than, as I shall argue a little later, on the continuation of what is normally experienced in the space of the political. It also makes 'a normally peaceful people' the agent of violence.

First, let me explain what I mean by 'political time'. In Sri Lanka, it is striking how long-term time-reckoning more generally is now politically inflected. In his essay on 'Biographies of the Nation State', which I discussed in the previous chapter, Uyangoda singles out the political violence of 1958 as the crucial temporal watershed in his childhood (Uyangoda 1997: 13). When I conducted oral historical interviews during my village fieldwork in the early 1980s, people spoke of the past as segmented in political terms: events located in the pre-Independence period were spoken of as 'British time' (*britanya kalaya*); this was followed by 'war time' (*yuddha kalaya*; i.e. Second World War), 'D. S. Senanayake's time', 'S. W. R. D. Banadaranaike's time', 'UNP time', and so on through the list of post-Independence leaders. Refugee accounts of the circumstances of their flight from Sri Lanka are usually peppered with the temporal markers left behind by the ebb and flow of the conflict: 'when the Indian Peace-keeping Force were here', 'when the Muslims were told to leave Jaffna'.

On the whole, Daniel's interview material avoids these temporal markers which fix particular incidents in a chronicle of political time, and which are central to most of the refugee narratives I have heard or read. In contrast to this, Daniel's reported narratives are often deprived of their expected moorings in political time. Some, it is true, refer to events like the 1983 violence itself, which position the moment of the tale well enough; but even then the reader is often left unclear about the political moment of the telling. It is quite possible that this feature of Daniel's book is quite unapparent to any reader who has not spent part of their life listening to Sri Lankans – in exile or at home, Sinhala and Tamil – talking of the troubles. But to anyone who has spent time engaged in conversations like this, this silence is oddly disturbing. The analytic effect of this mode of presentation is to abstract the victim from the political circumstances which produced their own victimhood, and thus to make a tale of particular suffering situated in a particular conflict into a larger allegory of suffering-in-general. To tell us what it means to be human, it seems we have to leave the political behind.

Daniel's apparent aversion to the political would appear to be prospective as much as retrospective, and it is based in an understandable pessimism about the future. For Daniel, as for many others, the best lack all conviction:

The moment a glimmer of a clear outline begins to take form, the present, with a bomb, a betrayal, an ambush, or an assassination, shatters the outline and scatters bits of the nascent image. Scholars gather in person or in their writings, sometimes pooling their thoughts in conferences or in edited volumes, attempting to rechart their own visions for the future. It all seems contrived and even hopeless. Only the naïve and the innocent pose the straightforward question: 'What is the solution?' An embarrassed hush falls upon a room filled with the seasoned, to be broken, after a trying pause, by someone who is willing to offer a polite, even if painfully inadequate, response. There are no clear answers, no clear visions. (Daniel 1996: 109)

Or, as Daniel puts in his Introduction, 'If there be solutions, they may well rest in forgetting the causes and remembering the carnage in "paradise"' (Daniel 1996: 9). In other words, the sequence of events, the particularities of the recent past, and the machinations of current politics, who-did-what-in-response-to-what, binds us to the renewal of the horror. If redemption is possible, it may come from a considered break with the particular – and with the political – leaving more time and space for attention to horror in the abstract.

Kapferer, in contrast, is keen to remind his readers that he is not indifferent to politics in general; 'The present disasters are born of historically produced political and social conditions' (Kapferer 1988: 22). But those conditions are mostly left unspecified. Indeed, when he strays dangerously close to a discussion of the specifically political dimension of the 1983 events, he is quick to dismiss the whole area of discussion:

There is a faintly hollow sound to statements that rioters were acting irrationally or were following political orders. There is evidence that much of the destruction was caused by organized gangs of hoodlums, some of which were actively encouraged by political leaders (Obeyesekere 1984). But none of this mitigates the fact that Tamils were for a while engulfed by the flames of a passionate Sinhalese Buddhist violence which was directed against them alone. (Kapferer 1988: 33)

In other words, to say rioters were acting as political agents is akin to simply saying they were acting 'irrationally': both explanations apparently constitute an explaining away of moral responsibility. For some reason, it is crucial to Kapferer that the violence be identified as '*Sinhala Buddhist violence*'.

Kapferer's argument is a familiar one in the recent literature on anthropology and violence. By stripping violence of its political context, much anthropological work either exoticizes or mystifies the topic. For example, in what amounts to a manifesto for violence as the new exotic in anthropology, Carolyn Nordstrom employs the textual oddity of a strikethrough across the word 'reason', and argues 'a concern with the reasons of war comes dangerously close to a concern with making war reasonable' (Nordstrom 1995: 138): explaining, she says, is too close to 'explaining away'. But this aversion to the language of cause and explanation is not so very far from common tabloid representations of other people's troubles: the 'deep' antipathies, the 'ancient' hatreds, the 'senseless' violence – violence which is employed, apparently, 'for its own sake'. It is true that most anthropologists working on this topic would be appalled by this particular language, but the rhetoric of 'horror', 'savagery', and 'chaos' found in much recent ethnography produces a similar mixture of enchantment and distance in the reader, while isolating the figure of the victim from the human actions and intentions which combined to create that victimhood in the first place.

All of which is in marked contrast to the pieces published by anthropologists, and other scholars, in the immediate aftermath of the 1983 violence. Immersed as they were in the flow of events, these were indeed often concerned with the causes of what had happened, and most converged on recent political history as the likeliest place to find such causes. All we know about the 1983 violence suggests that most of it was orchestrated by members of the ruling party, the UNP, and carried out by small gangs of party supporters, travelling in state-owned buses, and using typed electoral lists to identify (and attack) Tamil-owned property (Hoole 2001). For the perpetrators it was, politically speaking, business as usual: the same gangs had been used to rig a referendum victory in 1982, and the same routine, of using party supporters to target selected Tamil properties, had been employed on a smaller scale in one of the island's Provinces in 1981.

An eyewitness account by the French historian Eric Meyer stresses the prosaic quality of what happened much of the time:

The operations that I witnessed were methodically organized. Their leaders often dressed in European clothes and had written instructions and lists of places to attack. Groups of five or six youths in sarongs armed with Molotov cocktails would empty houses or shops of a part of their contents and set fire to them, continuing on their way forthwith, often by car. The looters from the nearest shanty town would then arrive whilst the generous distribution of arrack would help to maintain the excitement. (Meyer 1984: 139)

Not surprisingly, then, accounts by those who were closer to the violence itself present it in the context of longer-term trends in the country's politics. Gananath Obeyesekere's (1984) immediate reaction to the 1983 events (cited in the earlier quote from Kapferer) was to write a piece on 'The Origins and Institutionalisation of Political Violence'. In this article Obeyesekere recounts a string of incidents in the years leading up to the trouble, in which gangs of government supporters had employed violence against their political opponents.

In these early responses to the violence, the 'political' dimension was analysed in a relatively literal way: 'political' indicated actions by party members or supporters, working from instructions from known political figures as part of a co-ordinated action. But more recent research on memories of 1983 could usefully extend our understanding of the political dimension of these events. In the early 1990s, two Chicago-trained anthropologists, Pradeep Jeganathan and Malathi de Alwis, carried out fieldwork in a Colombo suburb. Jeganathan's work has concentrated on local idioms of masculinity, especially the image of the 'fearless' male invoked in local assessments of the actions of the kind of 'thug' involved in the political violence of the early 1980s. In a fascinating article (Jeganathan 1996), he explores the slow way in which local memories of the 1983 violence bubbled to the surface during his research. At first, he was told that nothing really happened in this area. Then he discovered that a single Tamil family had been driven from their home, and had subsequently emigrated to Australia. Some of those who recalled this event denied these people were especially targeted because of their 'Tamilness', hinting instead at other problems, and eventually a complex story of local animosities emerges. On the one hand the family who were victimized had fallen out with the neighbours over an accusation of theft against a neighbour's child. On the other, the local 'big family' of landlords had wanted them removed from their rented home for some time. The eventual attack on their house had little to do with 'politics' in the sense of national party politics, but, according to Jeganathan, a lot to do with politics in a broader sense. Depending on the perspective from which the tale was told, the attack was either a reaffirmation of local class hierarchies, within an idiom of shared Sinhala-ness, or a moment of egalitarian exhilaration in which the signs of inequality (in this case an expensive set of sanitary-ware in the bathroom) were smashed. The transgressive moment of violence was, for some at least, a moment of expanded possibility, when anything in the local order might be up for grabs: to echo West's informants in Mozambique (chapter four) 'anything can be said and anything can be done' (West 2005: 29). In the end, Jeganathan sees the stories he collected as moving back and forth across the same contradiction, between the ideal of modernity as a society of equals – he could as easily have glossed this as 'democracy' – and the impossible reality of inequality and exclusion.

The events of July 1983 did indeed shock many people, and there were ways in which what took place could be seen as unique and unprecedented. The events themselves, and the government's reaction to them, were the most important factors in swaying Tamils to the separatist cause in the middle 1980s. As a result, an unsavoury but containable dispute became a full-blown civil war. In the south, government opponents also learned from what happened, especially the realization that this government would, if pushed, take extreme steps to 'punish' those of its own people it felt to have stepped out of line. Yet the fact remains that, at the time, the violence seemed a logical, and almost predictable, outcome of a much longer process of politically generated violence: attacks on Tamils after the election victory in 1977; attacks on strikers in 1980; more attacks on Tamils during the local election campaign in 1981; attacks and intimidation of opposition activists in the referendum of 1982; attacks on political opponents in 1983; intimidation of judges after what was seen as an anti-government ruling (Hoole 2001). The micro-politics of particular acts in particular places, as explored by Jeganathan, are much the same as the micro-politics of electoral allegiance, in which political idioms are used to re-describe local animosities, and the energy of performative agonism is infused with the special flavour of local history and local resentments. If people measured their lives in political time, then violence had become like the ticking of a clock. Whatever the long-term consequences, as they happened the 1983 attacks on the Tamil minority were just another pulse in the rhythm of the political.

Towards a Topology of Violence

One simple way to demonstrate the political dimension of the 1983 violence would be to plot its occurrence in the part of Sri Lanka in which I was working at the time. All the major towns to the west of my fieldwork village – Balangoda, Pelmadulla, Kahawata, Ratnapura – were spared any significant violence or destruction. Visible signs of violence were easily to be seen to the north, south-west, and further west – in the hill towns of Bandarawela and Badulla, closer to the capital in Avissawella, and on the road to the south in Deniyaya. But if one were then to plot the violence that had occurred in this area in 1981, the towns 'spared' in 1983 are precisely the towns targeted on the earlier occasion. The neatness of the contrast is compelling evidence that the violence was carried out by the same perpetrators. The most plausible explanation for the pattern is this: the 1981 violence had been intended as a salutary warning to Tamils of what might happen if there were further trouble in the north; it was organized by a fraction within the ruling UNP, led by a leading Cabinet Minister, Cyril Mathew. The areas struck hardest in 1981 were the areas where this fraction had its strongest organizational base, and closest links to local police and administrators. The organizers of the 1983 violence did not bother to return to the sites of their earlier warning, but instead struck across a broader area which had been mostly left alone in 1981. A map of the 1981 and 1983 violence would also be a map of a political process.

Veena Das (Das 1996), in an important article about the 1984 anti-Sikh violence in Delhi, provides an even more striking example of a similar process. Das was one of a group of academic observers who made the first public reports of the scale of the violence and, crucially, of large-scale involvement of the ruling Congress Party in the organization and perpetration of the violence (Das *et al.* 1984). Working with students from the University in the weeks and months that followed the violence, she was able to combine practical engagement in rehabilitation work with wider surveys of the affected areas. One of the early products of this work was a remarkable essay, 'Our Work to Cry, your Work to Listen' (Das 1990b), which documented the predicament of survivors of the violence, especially widowed women who had escaped the vengeful rioters, only to have to deal with the complex patterns of a grief endlessly refracted through the often antagonistic expectations of affinity and gender. As well as containing heart-breakingly personal testimony, the essay moves effortlessly between the individual and the sociological, the personal work of grief and guilt and the collective work of mourning and remaking a social world which had been smashed.

Six years after 'Our Work to Cry', Das revisited material from the same research. In this second article, she uses material from her students' socio-economic survey of affected areas in Sultanpuri, a resettlement colony in the west of the city, to show the uneven distribution of the 1984 violence. In particular, one block (A/4) suffered a disproportionate share of the killings, while apparently similar areas were much more lightly affected. In order to understand how this came about, Das discusses the local economy, assesses possible tensions generated by the consumption style of the Sikhs in the worst-affected areas, but, most important of all, takes the reader into the world of local micro-politics. The residents of the worst-affected block had been in dispute with a local leader from a neighbouring block about their use of a parcel of land to build a *gurdwara* (Sikh temple). A few days before the assassination of Mrs Gandhi, there had been a fight between the leaders of the two blocks. On the night of the assassination itself there was some minor friction between the two blocks; the situation deteriorated when the two leaders, drunk, began to exchange insults. A little later, the neighbouring leader returned with a group of thirty or forty men from the neighbourhood. They were accompanied by the police and, somewhere in the background, was the local Congress Big Man, who Das simply identifies as 'X' in her article. The leader from A/4 who had been free with his insults earlier was the first to be targeted, along with his wife and sons. Similar sized groups returned the next morning, and again in the days that followed, taking out men to be killed, and looting the houses.

Das uses this evidence to make a number of theoretical points, not all of which I will pursue here. First of all, no explanation which simply attributes agency to 'the crowd' is going to explain the uneven pattern of violence. To understand this, we need to see the outbreak of violence as continuous with 'normal' social relations, not radically separate from them. After the assassination, the initial violence in block A/4 was an episode in an older quarrel, rooted in other more local concerns. Nevertheless this old quarrel, and the particular relations between local leaders and the shadowy Congress Big Man, set up predispositions for escalation which were less evident in otherwise comparable blocks. Local political antagonisms were recast in the language of national antagonisms; the capillaries of everyday agonism, which throughout this book I have called 'the political', become the channels for violence. What happens is not simply a reproduction of local structures of antagonism, but also an opportunity for a remaking of local social order. In that respect the violence, like the political more generally, is productive. And what Das calls in the title of her article 'the spatialization of violence' is also the spatialization of the political.

Violence and Sovereignty

Das' exploration of the local circumstances of urban violence is echoed in other important work in India. Here is the psycho-analyst Sudhir Kakar's description of a riot captain from a Muslim area of Hyderabad:

Unlike Majid Khan, Akbar is a true *pelhwan*. He has been trained as a wrestler since the age of ten and comes from a family where for the last four generations the men have all been wrestlers. Among the Hindus, he is notorious as a killer, while many Muslims approvingly acknowledge his role in the organization of the community's violence during the riots. Living in a large house with four wrestler brothers and their families, a widowed mother, and three wives, Akbar is a prosperous man who owns a hotel and three *taleemkhanas*, as the wrestling gymnasiums are called in Urdu. Like most other *pehlwans*, the chief source of his income is what the *pehlwans* delicately describe as 'land business'. (Kakar 1996: 59–60)

What, we may ask, is 'land business'? It is, according to Kakar, 'one of the outcomes of India's crumbling legal system' (Kakar 1996: 60). Because the courts are so slow and ineffectual in property cases, people increasingly have recourse to the use of specialist thugs, in this case wrestlers or *pehlwan*, in order to gain control of property they may have lost to a sitting tenant or be unable to take hold of by themselves. If both sides hire thugs, then it is simple enough for the thugs to agree an amicable solution between themselves, which they can then offer to their terrified employers. 'Overt violence', according to Kakar, is in fact 'rare in this informal system where a black legality, like a black economy, runs parallel to the state's legal system' (Kakar 1996: 60; cf. Brass 1997: 204–59).

Midway through her article, Das notes the presence of the police during the violence, their acquiescence in what was happening, and, in some cases, their active involvement in it: 'The implications of this for understanding the nature of the state in India', she notes (Das 1996: 184), 'are profound but not adequately theorized.' So what *are* the implications of this kind of evidence for our understanding of the postcolonial state in South Asia? Where Das discusses the 'informal economy', Kakar talks more starkly of a 'black legality' and a 'black economy'. In the article I discussed in the previous chapter, Gupta (1995) draws our attention to what he calls the performative dimensions of the state, and it is easy enough to think of other examples – the complex staging and artifice of a court of law, for example. But in Kakar's example, the courts themselves seem to *operate*, but not to *function*: actually to achieve results in a dispute, more and more people have to take recourse to 'black legality'. For people in this position, the official courts are arenas for performances, and

apparently little else. Discussing the views of villagers from two different villages on an incident involving the local police, the veteran North
Indian fieldworker Paul Brass offers the following summary:

The accounts given by villagers from Pachpera and Manauli suggest that they
both have a similar perspective on the realities of law and order and political
life in the countryside, which contain two salient features. One is that there is
no law and order in the countryside. Rather there are sets of forces operating
in pursuit of their own interests, which include *dacoits*, police, villagers who
belong to distinct castes and communities, and politicians. These forces do
not operate on opposite sides of a dichotomous boundary separating the
mechanisms of law and order from those of criminals, but are integrated in
relationships in which criminal actions bring some or all of them into play
with unpredictable results. In this context, a criminal act does not necessarily
or even likely lead to a police investigation, a report, the filing of a case, pursuit
of the criminals, and their being hauled up before a court. Rather, it provides
an occasion for the testing of relationships and alliances or for the forming
of new ones. In the ensuing encounters, force and violence are always a
possibility. (Brass 1997: 75)

In so far as 'law and order' has any presence in this area it is, according to
Brass, as a rhetorical device, something to which policemen or bureaucrats may appeal in constructing their version of contentious incidents.
As for judges and courts, 'Law and the judiciary as abstractions have
little meaning in rural north India, where lawyers and judges are highly
politicized and judicial decisions are often for sale' (Brass 1997: 92). In the
conclusion to the book, Brass develops and assesses his self-consciously
Hobbesian vision of rural India at war with itself, with police, politicians, and criminals bound into 'networks of power relations', frequently
accompanied by the use of violence (Brass 1997: 275).

It should be swiftly pointed out that, whatever the merits of Brass'
Hobbesian interpretation of the Utar Pradesh countryside, it is supported by some remarkably detailed ethnography. His analytic thrust
is not so much to attack the liberal pretensions of the Indian state as to

challenge the prevailing wisdom on the pattern of collective violence in North India. Violence in itself, in a setting like this, is relatively unremarkable, but some moments of violence take on a new life as part of the politics of *stories about* violence. Indeed, as he demonstrates, stories about violence can even circulate tellingly when there is no evidence that violence has ever occurred. His account, then, is an account of the politics of violence in a world of amoral politicians, thuggish policemen, and opportunistic peasants. What is important for our purposes is not so much his attack on primordialist approaches to collective violence, still less his conventionally instrumental version of local politics, but his remarkably rich and nuanced depiction of the mysteries of law and order in rural North India. Anecdotal evidence suggests that many other ethnographers might endorse Brass' force-field account of the police and their various potential antagonists in the countryside, and only timidity has prevented us from documenting this aspect of the postcolonial state more comprehensively.[4]

Whatever else we may conclude, it is clear that a straightforward imputation of 'externality' to the state vis-à-vis society, whether expressed in cultural, political, or religious terms, is the exception rather than the rule. Indeed the theoretical description of the state as 'outside' society, and exercising a special kind of domination over it, could be plausibly argued to be another example of Mitchell's 'state-effect'. The state is not *experienced* simply as an abstraction, or as a separate 'thing' clearly marked off from the equally separate and autonomous space of 'society'. Secondly, the necessary existence of social relations across the putative state–society boundary is a powerful entropic factor in the social world as a whole, blurring the boundaries yet more, but all the while making performances of 'state-ness' ever more necessary.

---

[4] In this respect, Paul Alexander's analysis of a southern fishing village in Sri Lanka in the early 1970s, originally published in 1982, was unusually prescient in its documentation of the ubiquity of everyday violence (Alexander 1995).

A major problem with some of the analyses presented so far is that they frequently depend on a more or less articulated contrast with a normative model of a singular liberal state. The examples of local violence – whether it be sporadic, large-scale communal violence, or persistent, everyday violence – are presented either as departures from the expected shape of the political order, or simply negations of it ('the complete breakdown of law and order'). The main intellectual challenge to this implicit model of the state is the Foucaultian vision of modern technologies of power, working their way through whole populations, as part of the new order of postcolonial governmentality. It is hard, though, to make sense of Brass' account of the North Indian countryside in these terms – though this has not stopped Brass trying – or to use this frame to interpret the workings of political violence in a place like Sultanpuri. In Foucault's teleology, modern biopower *replaces* spectacular violence in Europe at some point in the eighteenth century. But in postcolonial South Asia, apparently, the spectacle of violence endures.

There is, though, another, intellectually more radical, way in which we might approach the distribution of violence in postcolonial society. This is in terms of sovereignty. In his *Homo Sacer*, Giorgio Agamben (1998) revisits and revises Foucault's account of the rise of modern biopower. Through a re-reading of classical sources, he challenges Foucault's argument for the novelty of modern power working at the level of what he translates as 'bare life'. At the root of Western ideas of sovereignty is the Roman figure of *homo sacer*, the sacred man who 'may be killed and yet not sacrificed' (Agamben 1998: 8). In commentaries upon earlier arguments by Schmitt (Schmitt 1996 [1932]) and Benjamin (Benjamin 1979 [1920/1]), Agamben argues that sovereign power is founded in the transgressive taking of 'bare life': violence and law are, from their very inception, conjoined. What differs about modern forms of power is not the workings of power at the level of the body, but rather the democratic aspiration to make the bodies of all men and women the subjects, rather than the objects, of political power.

Agamben's argument is, to put it mildly, dense and abstract, but it allows him to make important analytic connections in his understanding of modern forms of political order. The Nazi death-camps – always, one suspects, in the back of Foucault's mind, but rarely explicitly invoked – become the central paradigm for Agamben's argument about the workings of modern power and sovereignty. Issues of life and death become central to all forms of sovereignty, although the democratic transition brings to light distinctive tensions and contradictions. We can, then, talk in the same terms about the institutional order of modern power, and the subjective dispositions of modern political agents; we can link the formal institutions of the state with the everyday technologies of biopower which Foucault concentrated on; and we can be at once alert to the rational murmurings of everyday bureaucracy, without discounting the enduring importance of the spectacular. It does this in part by making the topographic puzzle – what is 'inside' and what is 'outside' sovereign power – the central issue. Sovereignty is founded in this moment of puzzle: the need to step 'outside' the realm of law in order to make the law.

Perhaps most importantly for any new anthropology of the political, Agamben's argument successfully dissolves the hard-and-fast divide between the traditional and the modern, thus allowing us to get a better handle on the enduring potency of older languages of politics and power, without simply placing them 'outside' the modern political order. To follow this example, I suspect, we may not need to invest too heavily in Agamben's own philological researches into Greek and Roman texts on sovereignty, still less his quaint attachment to late nineteenth-century anthropology. The importance of ideas of life and sacrifice in his conclusions provides fertile ground for a re-reading of classical anthropological and historical texts on kingship, most obviously Kantorowicz (1958), whom he cites, but also Hocart (1970), whom he does not. It is quite easy to imagine an anthropological account of sovereignty, based for example on ethnographic understandings of African or Southeastern Asian idioms of power, easily surpassing the narrowly Eurocentric genealogy employed by Agamben. Hansen (2005), for example, supplements his account of Agamben's argument, with a short summary of Sahlins' well-known essay on the Stranger-king, an essay which explores Polynesian and African examples of the link between power and violent transgression (Sahlins 1985). There is much work to be done here, but the fact remains that Agamben has identified certain key dynamics in the operations of sovereignty – the place of violence, the 'state of exception' – which neither liberal political theory, nor Foucaultian poststructuralism, can adequately capture.

Hansen has made a brilliant contribution to this task in a sweeping essay, which interprets some of the more striking features of BJP governance in India within the framework of a new synoptic account of the distribution of sovereignty in colonial and postcolonial India (Hansen 2005). Hansen makes creative use of Agamben's ideas to separate sovereignty from the state, to recognize potentially plural forms of sovereignty as co-existing in the same social space, and to treat violence as a key diagnostic for mapping these different manifestations of sovereignty. He detects three different ideas of sovereignty at work in postcolonial India, each with a rather different genealogy behind it: the formal legal sovereignty of the state and its institutions; the moral sovereignty of the nation, still often imagined as somehow outside or separate from the formal state apparatus; and the dispersed, local centres of sovereignty, based on local Big Men and their command of everyday violence and the perfomance of political spectacle. We can see how events like the 1984 violence in Delhi involve the interplay of all three kinds of sovereignty: the policemen assisting the rioters 'in the name of the law', the moral call to the nation in the rioters' cries about the death of Indira, and the clusters and capillaries of local politics and everyday violence. We can also better understand some of the ambivalence of politically successful right-wing groups like Shiv Sena who at times feel the need to reassert their oppositional position outside the formal structures they now control.

Perhaps most importantly we can begin to make better sense of people like the LTTE cadres and Khalistan activists I quoted at the start of the previous chapter. The language of love and destruction, their apparent fixation with redemptive violence, no longer look as odd as they did earlier. Minimally, they can now be interpreted as experiments in popular sovereignty, attempts to build a new political order from the endlessly reiterated act of sacrifice. Obviously, at this stage in the argument, this is not an intellectual solution to the mystery presented by these movements: much more detailed work needs to be done on the history, politics, political economy and sociology of each movement. But situating them in the light of wider evidence about the distribution of violence in the postcolonial political order makes their actions and ideas seem much less aberrant. Agamben's reworking of central notions of sovereignty, violence, and law can then provide a theoretical complement to this empirical work, again by helping us to see such movements not so much as departures from the liberal norm, but better as extreme cases which in their very exaggeration help us better understand the dynamics and possibilities of everyday violence and everyday politics.

A Coda on Hope

These two chapters do not exhaust the topic of the developing anthropology of the state, but the sombre note in this one is rather more one-sided than it should be. If we want to understand why the fighters of the LTTE want a state of their own, then there are other factors – some positive, some negative – to consider. High among the negative factors is the long history of brutalization from the agents of the actually existing state: a state of one's own would, in the rebel imagination, be a state whose subjects were free from attack, detention, and torture. High among the positive factors would be the remarkable record of the Sri Lankan state in addressing basic needs in the 1950s and 1960s, such that by the outbreak of the civil war, Sri Lankan figures for literacy and life expectancy were close to those found in Western Europe, despite a vastly lower per capita GDP.

For much of the postcolonial period, across South Asia the state has represented above all an instrument for the achievement of social justice. As Sunil Khilnani puts it:

[After Independence] the state was enlarged, its ambitions inflated, and it was transformed from a distant, alien object into one that aspired to infiltrate the everyday lives of Indians, proclaiming itself responsible for everything they could desire: jobs, ration cards, educational places, security, cultural recognition. The state thus etched itself into the imagination of Indians in a way that no previous political agency had ever done. (Khilnani 1997: 41)

For the villagers in Sri Lanka I worked with in the 1980s, the state was generally perceived as a source of resources (jobs, healthcare, land, contracts), a source of social capital (the prestige that follows either possession of a job, or exploitation of a privileged link to local politicians or officials), a source of oppression (the venal activities of the police), an arena for disputes (the courts, selective appeal to the police), and a screen on to which villagers could project their visions of their own future. It should be clear that shorthand allusions to 'the state' or even 'the local state' cover a multitude of different institutions, practices, and representations. But, within this multitude, there lies a simple truth: for these villagers, 'the state' has made an enormous difference, mostly for the good although often enough for ill, to the quality of their lives.

Sudipta Kaviraj, in an important essay on the 'culture of representative democracy', reminds us that democracy is 'after all, a way of imagining the world' (Kaviraj 1998: 148). Here the state becomes a much more potentially productive resource in social life: at its most alluring, a ground of utopian possibility; more mundanely a place you go when you are ill, or the harvest fails. Even the most disappointed and cynical of observers usually still works with the ideal that the state is, or should be, a source of justice and redress (however remote that possibility may be in practice for most of its citizens). But there is always the sense of ambivalence (to use Alter's (1993) term): to engage with the state is to engage with the world of 'dirty politics'; to be aware of its 'sublime' qualities, of rationality and justice, is to be reminded of its 'profane' failings in the world of dirty politics, to employ a distinction from Hansen (2001a: 35–8). There are two possible responses to this ambivalence. One is that kind of self-making which is intentionally opposed to the profane failings of the political order (Alter's wrestlers, the Muslim reformers of the Tabligh-i-Jamaat I discuss in the next chapter). Another is a commitment to a radical cleansing of the profane aspects of the state and the political, a project Hansen calls 'anti-politics': 'To denounce *rajkaraan* (politics), to separate the nation and its cultures from the realm of rational statecraft, and to adopt a moral, antipolitical critique of political leaders is possibly the most legitimate and the most common oppositional stance in contemporary India' (Hansen 2001b: 229). Here we might be reminded of another of Kaviraj's (1998) implications of democracy, what he calls its 'plasticity', but which from another point of view we might call its culture of uncertainty and indeterminacy.

This also brings me back full circle to the question of violence. The Sri Lankan youth groups, the LTTE and the JVP, both work, or worked, in this cleansing space of 'anti-politics'. The LTTE, in particular, has shown itself fascinated with the redemptive possibilities of death and violence, in a kind of secular soteriology: 'We are happy at the thought of our death in battle', as the young cadre put it to Trawick, 'because then we become part of history.' For them the sublime vision of the state-to-be retains its purity because it is always and endlessly deferred. Life and death, the pure and the impure – the 'ambivalence' of the state as imaginative field challenges the prosaic categories of conventional political analysis.

SEVEN

Pluralism in Theory, Pluralism in Practice

'Political theory, which presents itself as addressing universal and abiding matters ... the truth about things as at bottom they always and everywhere necessarily are, is in fact and inevitably, a specific response to immediate circumstances' (Geertz 2000: 218). Or so Clifford Geertz reminds us at the start of his recent summary of culture and politics in the post-1989 world. His scepticism towards the universal claims of political theory is not new. Radcliffe-Brown's dismissal of the state as a problem was part and parcel of a wholesale dismissal of the relevance of political philosophy to political anthropology, a position eagerly endorsed by his editors on that occasion (Fortes and Evans-Pritchard 1940).

The problem for anthropology is not so much that theory remains covertly rooted in the particulars of its own political place and its own political time. Nor is it the lofty confusion of universal predicaments with local circumstances. (How could an anthropologist object to *this*?) Problems start to pile up when the naïve reader fails to identify the particular origins of a theoretical stance. Foucault's theoretical positions should seem weird to a reader ignorant of the political-intellectual world of 1960s Paris, and the twin shadows of the authoritarian French Communist Party (PCF), and the self-dramatizing figure of Jean-Paul Sartre, against whom so much of his work was directed. (Its subsequent smooth translation to Reagan's America in the 1980s is a mystery I leave for future intellectual historians.) The political philosophy of multiculturalism and minority rights, with which this chapter is concerned, often seems implausibly liberal and fair-minded, until you realize that this is a literature dominated by the writings of impeccably liberal and fair-minded Canadians.

More recently the recent vogue for Agamben's work raises the obvious question: what is theory *for* in any anthropology of the political? Agamben's work, after all, is in places obscure, irredeemably European in its intellectual and political orientation, and, until very recently, was completely ignored by anthropologists. Reading anthropological responses to his work can be quite puzzling. Hansen, in the paper discussed in the previous chapter, focuses tightly on the question of 'sovereign violence' (Hansen 2005), and uses this to map a broad sweep of colonial and postcolonial political history. In contrast, Caroline Humphrey, enjoined to write on 'Sovereignty' in the recent Nugent and Vincent *Companion* (Nugent and Vincent 2004), provides a fascinating account of emergent political order in a post-Soviet urban space. She downplays the centrality of violence and instead counterposes 'ways of life' – pre-existent and ethnographically documented – to what she describes as the 'thin' account of sovereignty in Agamben's own work (Humphrey 2004). Both Hansen and Humphrey use Agamben's arguments to bring out the potential plurality of sovereignty in 'transitional' (postcolonial, post-Soviet) settings: a sense of '*the* state' as a singular presence is inevitably (and, I think, helpfully) undermined by this move. In contrast, Das and Poole, in a thoughtful critical review of Agamben's arguments, focus more on the 'state of exception'. In particular they emphasize the way in which the processes of violent exclusion and inclusion remain at the heart of modern state practices. They also echo other anthropologists' dissatisfaction with Agamaben's light empirical touch. But in their account, whatever the diversity of practices encountered in the exercise of sovereignty, they all point back to 'the state', and 'the state' itself remains resolutely singular (Das and Poole 2004). All three arguments bring out facets of Agamben's work and apply them illuminatingly, even if an untutored observer might come away quite confused by the different directions the authors follow from ostensibly the same source.

Pluralism in Practice

A 'scientific' anthropology of the political, as envisaged by Radcliffe-Brown and his students, and scrupulously free of the fanciful imaginings of the philosophers, would be a desperately miserable creature. But so too would a theoretically correct anthropology, in which what ethnography there was, found itself shoehorned into the pre-fabricated compartments ordained by an empirically challenged philosopher. The relationship between theory and ethnography in this area should be at once productive and suspicious. This chapter is structured as an exercise in examining the relationship between theory and ethnography. It also sees a partial return to the questions which dominated the first part of this book: How do we understand culture and cultural difference? What are the political consequences of different ways of construing cultural pluralism? My argument here is driven by a certain frustration, because theoretical argument in this area has been dominated by extraordinarily naïve models of cultural difference and cultural identity. I start with a restatement of certain classic anthropological arguments about culture and pluralism – Ethnicity 101 for political philosophers, if you like. The second and third sections of the chapter are based on a comparison between the fate of pluralism in Sri Lanka and India. In India a limited legal pluralism (the continued recognition of Muslim family law) has been the focus of repeated attacks from the Hindu right, attacks which have led to a debate about the viability of any kind of pluralism in a modern or postcolonial nation-state. In Sri Lanka, despite the war, the country's highly pluralistic legal code has been barely noticed, either by religious chauvinists or by academic commentators. The conclusion returns to ethnography and violence, and the corrosive effect of violence on everyday civility.

I start with two – possibly somewhat unexpected – examples from the work of anthropologists. The first is a village called Hpalang, as described by Edmund Leach on the basis of fieldwork in a remote area of highland Burma, before and during the Second World War. This 'village' had about 500 people, or 130 households, living in 9 hamlets, and speaking 6 different languages or dialects. In 1940 about one fifth of the population had converted to Christianity, but this Christian minority was already pretty equally divided between Catholics and Baptists. Although Leach provides very little sense of how this extraordinary polyglot collectivity got along on an everyday basis, he provides one fact which is crucial to his eventual analysis: all the groups not merely intermarry, they intermarry in a sociologically coherent way. Moreover, according to Leach, they all participate in the same political games – games in which marriage, and the manipulation of marks of cultural difference, both feature prominently (Leach 1954).

For my second example I must shift continents and time-frames, from the fringes of British rule in Southeast Asia at the end of the colonial era, to the centre of postcolonial Britain, Southall in the 1980s. Southall is a suburb of 60,000 people, who live in the shadow of Heathrow airport on the western edge of London. Within the overwhelmingly diasporic population of Southall, it is possible to delineate a number of what are conventionally called 'communities': Hindus, Muslims, Sikhs – all with historical origins in the Indian subcontinent – as well as Afro-Caribbeans and Whites (of whom a substantial minority are of Irish origin). In a wonderfully subtle analysis, Gerd Baumann has investigated the ways in which young people of all communities use apparently common kinship idioms – specifically a rather elastic reference to 'cousins' – in negotiating their relations with each other. The origins of this usage appear to lie with one particularly dominant group, whose kinship discourse provides, in Baumann's terms, a 'hegemonic' point of reference for youth of all communities. Interestingly the group in question are not the Whites but the Punjabis (Baumann 1995).

What links these examples is obviously the notion of pluralism, and particularly the strange things that happen when self-evidently plural social settings are subject to close anthropological or ethnographic attention. First of all, both Leach and Baumann are deeply sceptical of purely cultural accounts of cultural difference. Leach's *Political Systems of Highland Burma* is, among many other things, a sustained attack on the view of 'cultures' as discrete, bounded, and internally homogeneous. Interestingly, the villains of Leach's piece are not American cultural anthropologists, but colonial ethnologists with an eager proclivity to map linguistic differences on to cultural units which then reappear as tribes, races or communities. In all the talk about head-dresses and turbans, it is worth dwelling on one paragraph from Leach's Introduction:

In any geographical area which lacks fundamental natural frontiers, the human beings in adjacent areas of the map are likely to have relations with one another – at least to some extent – no matter what their cultural attributes may be. In so far as these relations are ordered and not wholly haphazard there is implicit in them a social structure. But, it may be asked, if social structures are expressed in cultural symbols, how can the structural relations between groups of different culture be expressed at all? *My answer to this is that the maintenance and insistence upon cultural difference can itself become a ritual action expressive of social relations.* (Leach 1954: 17)

The obvious point to be drawn from this paragraph is Leach's strong restatement of the contrast between the 'cultural' and the 'structural', and his insistence on the analytic necessity to subordinate the details of culture to the clarifying potential of social structure – a common and somewhat predictable move in the British anthropology of the time. But there is another point, less obvious but possibly as valuable: that the kind of pluralism he describes in Hpalang is no freakish occurrence, but can be safely assumed to be the normal human state of affairs: 'In any geographical area which lacks fundamental natural frontiers, the human beings in adjacent areas of the map are likely to have relations with one another.' What Leach does not make explicit here, but which seems an attractive corollary of his argument, is the idea that what we might call 'cultural monism' – the notion that any particular group of people are living in a non-plural world – is not the taken-for-granted, default mode of human existence. It is actually quite unusual, and rather than being taken for granted, always requires some kind of active explanation (from passing anthropologists), as well as some kind of active maintenance (by the monadic inhabitants of this zone of unanimity and unreflective tradition).

What of Baumann's example? First of all, in the spirit of Leach, he challenges what he calls the idea of the 'ethnic-as-cultural closure' in the study of postmigration communities. In other words, 'ethnic groups' (or 'minorities' or 'communities') do not live in sealed bubbles, closed off from the wider culture around them. And, rather like Leach, he shows how a sociologically intelligible account can be produced once the anthropologist abandons an attachment to the image of a world of discrete, culturally bounded, ethnic bubbles. Unlike Leach, though, he is in the end still interested in culture (rather than 'structure' in Leach's sense of hard, acultural social structure). What flow across the imaginary boundaries between Southall's ethnic groups are not necessarily – or not just – 'social relations' but *ideas about* social relations. And what begins to appear in Baumann's analysis is a new cultural field, cutting across differences of religion, language, or historical origin, shared by young people as they interact with each other. In short, here we gain a rare empirical sighting of that intellectually rather fashionable item: culture as emergent or evanescent, contested as much as shared. We also get something more, because, of course, everyone in Southall knows about 'culture' and 'cultural difference'. In a world of explicit talk about the 'multicultural' many, even most, young people think of themselves as 'naturally' divided by culture. Within this world of natural divisions, 'kinship', 'family', or 'blood' stands as a zone of certainty. Kinship is the given, the certain, even though it is known that it is given differently to different cultures. Because 'it's natural to do what your culture tells you to do', 'People can thus comprehend their lives as an enactment of consciously "cultural" specificities, and yet at the same time believe that all kinship, just like all culture, is "natural"' (Baumann 1995: 736). And, in a final paradoxical twist, these *ideas about* difference, culture, nature, and kinship are part of the shared, emergent culture of young Southallians, even as they 'do' kinship in different ways.

One final point of comparison. Both these accounts of what we might call the micro-politics of pluralism are structured with a strong sense of political or political-economic context. Specifically, both authors are aware of the role that the state, and its agents, play in these pluralistic contexts. For Leach, Hpalang's position close to the Chinese border, and far from the centres of power, was one important contextual factor in understanding its extreme cultural diversity (Leach 1954: 70–1). The highlands were politically remote, and culturally plural; down in the valleys, people sowed rice, professed Buddhism, and tended to be more unambiguously identified with the dominant Shan (Scott 1998: 196–7). Although Southall is in no sense on the fringe of the British state, for Baumann local uses of words like 'culture' and 'community' – which he italicizes as indigenous terms throughout his monograph *Contesting Culture* (Baumann 1996) – are part of broader official idioms of difference, propagated by the state through its local agents. They are, moreover, terms which share the same colonial provenance as the divisions of community or tribe or race which Leach railed against in Burma (Baumann 1996: 28–30). More generally we owe the very idea of a 'plural society' to Furnivall's analysis of colonial Burma and Indonesia, and its subsequent development to M. G. Smith's analysis of the diasporic societies of the Caribbean. It is, one could say, an earlier example of the drift of 'ideas about social relations' across apparent cultural and political boundaries. But from these and other cases, it has become clear that there is little point in talking about 'pluralism' without also talking about the politics (or possibly the political economy) of pluralism (Vincent 1996a).

Let me summarize the points I hope to have established from this comparison of two such apparently different cases. First of all, pluralism was not discovered yesterday, or even at some uncertain point in the 1980s – by James Clifford (1988) or Ulf Hannerz (1992) or even Arjun Appadurai (1990), however much these authors have done to put it back on the academic agenda – but has been an accepted part of anthropological analysis for at least fifty years. Secondly, self-conscious pluralism raises important issues about the intelligibility – or unintelligibility – of accounts or explanations which are themselves phrased in cultural terms. Faced with situations like those in Southall or Hpalang, analysts have to step back from the temptations of the monist fallacy – that is, the desire to treat the ethnographic universe as singular and ethnically or culturally bounded – and instead look at a broader social field, encompassing apparently different cultural units. The self-evident sociological coherence that emerges from such a perspective is not an artefact of clever academic trickery.

Just as people in South Asia still manage to marry their 'cousins' – in other words to 'do' what anthropologists have ponderously described as Dravidian kinship – without complex diagrams to refer to, so people everywhere 'do' cultural pluralism. That is they mostly make their way intelligibly enough through culturally plural settings, and in doing so, they must at times make use of some level of shared (meta-cultural) understanding of what is expected and legitimate in their apparently 'cross-cultural' social relations. One of the great virtues of Baumann's work is his documentation and analysis of this emergent level of shared understanding.

Put most generally, anthropologists' best efforts at dealing with pluralism have been based on scrupulous ethnographic attention to social fields in which agents are themselves conscious of the plural nature of their cultural context. Theoretically, Baumann's work suggests there is still mileage in the kind of political sociology of cultural difference proposed by Leach, especially if we drop or modify Leach's hard distinction between the fixed truths of social structure and the contingencies of culture. But if pluralism really is ubiquitous, we need to know when and why it becomes identified as an object of special concern. We need more processual accounts of the pluralizing strategies adopted by different agents in different settings, as well as an understanding of the institutions which reproduce an awareness of pluralism as a political issue. Not to mention, of course, the political institutions and political strategies and counter-strategies which attempt to render purity and singularity out of the great muddle of the plural.

The Political Production of 'Pluralism'

The issue of pluralism came to the top of the political agenda all over the South Asian subcontinent, just as one version of it – usually glossed as multiculturalism – has dominated recent political theory, especially in North America. The best-known examples of the theoretical interest in pluralism as a political problem are probably Charles Taylor's *Multiculturalism and 'The Politics of Recognition'* (Taylor 1992) and John Rawls' *Political Liberalism* (Rawls 1993). Rawls, for example, defines his central problem as 'How is it possible that there may exist over time a stable and just society of free and equal citizens profoundly divided by reasonable though incompatible religious, philosophical, and moral doctrines?' (Rawls 1993: xx). Clearly, the problem thus defined seems to chime with recent experiences in the world of South Asian politics. In India, the specific arguments raised by the Shah Bano case, and the broader debate about the possibility or impossibility of secularism as a political goal, would seem to focus on the difficulties of reconciling the interests and ideas of different, religiously defined, groups with quite irreconcilable notions of what is good and desirable, notions rooted in their own distinctive histories and forms of life. Indian problems, then, would seem to be Rawlsian, at least at the level of pure theory. Sri Lankan problems, in slight contrast, would seem to be more Taylorian – what divides Sinhala from Tamil are not necessarily 'incompatible religious, philosophical, and moral doctrines' (as a quick glance at the copious literature on religious change will confirm (e.g., Gombrich and Obeyesekere 1988)), so much as what Taylor calls 'the search for recognition and respect' and the collective hurt occasioned by misrecognition and disrespect (Taylor 1992: 70).

Yet, for all my admiration for the work of writers like Rawls and Taylor, I find their accounts of pluralism and multiculturalism oddly unreal. In particular, the philosophers' version of the plural society seems, in the light of ethnography like that just discussed, politically and sociologically very naïve. The recent 'cultural turn' in political theory has been remarkably uncritical about what we might mean by 'a culture'. From the right, Samuel Huntington effortlessly elides 'cultures' with 'civilizations', issues of 'identity' and 'common objective elements', in support of his celebrated hypothesis that, in the future, 'the dominating source of conflict will be cultural' (Huntington 1993: 22–5). Meanwhile, a liberal theorist like Kymlicka is equally confident about the self-evident existence of discrete 'cultures': 'I am using "a culture" as synonymous with "a nation" or "a people" – that is, as an intergenerational community, more or less institutionally complete, occupying a given territory or homeland, sharing a distinct language and history' (Kymlicka 1995: 18).

But theorists need to query some of the big substantives – culture, community, the state, the nation – that pepper their theorizing. Too often we concede too much too soon in our thinking about these entities. Here it is worth repeating a point from Brubaker's critique of 'methodological nationalism' in the study of nationalism:

'Nation' is a category of practice, not (in the first instance) a category of analysis. To understand nationalism, we have to understand the practical uses of the category 'nation', the ways it can come to structure perception, to inform thought and experience, to organize discourse and political action. (Brubaker 1996: 7; cf. Wimmer and Glick Schiller 2002)

So, too, for 'culture' and 'community', even perhaps 'pluralism' itself. Yet at the same time, we need to avoid the facile wishing away of real problems by categorizing the actors' perspective as fantasy (and thus irrelevant). It is true that we – disengaged academic observers – may find it difficult to isolate some shared 'thing' called 'Sinhala' or 'Tamil' culture, the 'Hindu' or 'Muslim' way of life, 'English values', or 'Scottish culture'. This does not mean that the people around us are simply deluded in their concerns for what they see as threats to their culture or their way of life, whether these come in the form of court decisions, or more brutal reminders of their place in the scheme of things. Yet, as Zizek (1993: 201) reminds us, when asked to elaborate on what constitutes this 'thing' that we feel is so central and valuable, we alternate between tautology and contradiction, at best invoking 'disconnected fragments' of the ways in which 'our' community organizes – feasts and ceremonies, whom you marry and how you mark it, the 'position of women' in your households (to cite some well-known South Asian criteria). The relationship between fragments and the elusive 'thing' is a *political* relationship. It follows that people's perceptions of their situation as 'culturally plural' are not the *a priori* foundation for particular styles of politics, so much as the *products* of those styles of politics. Once again, politicians' use of the rhetoric of deep-seated cultural difference should not be read as straightforward evidence for the empirical existence of such differences.

Sri Lanka is a striking case in point. A brief history of the Sri Lankan catastrophe is relatively easy to tell. It starts with the first mass elections seventy years ago, and ends with the civil war between the Sri Lankan state, perceived by some to be dominated by the majority Sinhala population, and the secessionist LTTE, based among the Tamil population of the island's north and east. Unlike its large neighbour to the north, Sri Lanka never developed a mass anti-colonial nationalist movement. Instead it was the site of one of Asia's earliest experiments with universal franchise, an experiment that was memorably opposed – because 'the people' were unready for such a responsibility – by the more vociferous elements of the elite-dominated Ceylon National Congress. In 1927, Sidney Webb, the Colonial Secretary, sent a Special Commission from London to investigate possible political reform in the colony. The only plausible nationalist party, the Ceylon National Congress, in its appearance before the Commission, argued forcefully for a strict income restriction on the franchise: 'If they went a grade lower, the delegation asserted, there was the danger that they might get a class of persons who would not use their votes with any sense of responsibility and whose votes might be at the disposal of the highest bidder' (de Silva 1973: 493). Worse still, some of the Congress leaders – apparently unaware of the expectations raised by the label 'nationalist' – refused to endorse a move towards self-government as a reasonable political goal (de Silva 1973: 494).

The Commission ignored them, and recommended the introduction of a new constitution, partly modelled on the structure of the then London County Council, with elections based on universal adult suffrage. Tamil politicians in the north boycotted the first elections under the new system in 1931, while elite Sinhala politicians, like the young and ambitious S. W. R. D. Bandaranaike, quickly shed their Christian upbringing and re-presented themselves as what became known as 'Donoughmore Buddhists'. Reflecting on the position of those elite politicians, reluctantly adjusting to a new form of mass politics, it is hard to think of a more apt illustration of Tom Nairn's description of the bourgeoisie's need 'to invite the masses into history' with an invitation written 'in a language they understood' (Nairn 1981: 340). The 'language they understood', as it emerged and coagulated in the political rhetoric of the 1930s, was a language of linguistic and religious identity, laced with experiments in xenophobia directed at different minorities: Indian Tamil labourers on the tea estates and Malayali immigrants in Colombo in particular. The distribution of population, and the constituency-based system of representation, resulted in two political zones: a zone of permanent opposition in the north, where Tamil parties dominated, and a zone of competition in the south, where (mostly Sinhala) politicians fought for the votes that would get them close to government (Russell 1982; Jayawardena 1985). The fault-lines established in the electoral politics of the 1930s became the disputed borderlands in the civil war fifty years later.

I doubt that any serious analyst would claim that the 'stuff' of cultural nationalism in Sri Lanka was simply made up in the political crucible of 1930s mass politicking. Some of it was quite old, some quite new, and quite a bit was borrowed from elsewhere. What interests me most about this now, though, is not the increasingly arid arguments about the relative antiquity of some sense of Sinhala Buddhist identity – arguments which have dominated the subliterature on the Sri Lankan crisis since the mid-1980s; I am rather more interested in the ways in which a sense of what it means to be Sinhala or Buddhist or Tamil or Muslim was transmuted in the new circumstances of mass politics, and the curious mixture of self-interest and transcendence, agonism and community, that is braided so tightly in the so-called 'politics of identity'. Nevertheless my crucial point is that, up to the 1980s at least, the history of 'identity politics' in Sri Lanka is first and foremost a *political* history.

Pluralism and the Legal Order

In 1985 the Supreme Court of India was called upon to adjudicate the case of Shah Bano, the elderly divorced wife of a Muslim advocate. At issue was the continued provision of maintenance. Shah Bano's former husband claimed to have made appropriate payments under the provisions of Islamic law; Shah Bano's lawyers argued that her husband was still liable to provide support, but under a section of the Criminal Procedures Act intended to force relatives to support otherwise destitute members of their families. The judges found in Shah Bano's favour, precipitating a wave of protest from Muslim groups, for whom the continued existence of their own code of personal law had long since become a central index of their collective self-esteem in the Indian nation-state. In response to this protest, Rajiv Gandhi's government allowed the passage of the Muslim Women (Protection of Rights on Divorce) Bill, a law which, of course, closed off the right of Muslim women to appeal, as Shah Bano had done, to the Criminal Procedure Code for maintenance.

This, in turn, further hardened the position of the Hindu right, who made the need for a single civil code a central plank in their platform of complaint against the supposedly 'privileged' position of minority groups like Muslims. Feminists who had, for very different reasons, also argued in the past for a more liberal and even civil code found themselves discomfited by the appearance of such unwelcome new allies from the right.

The case, and its implications, have generated a huge subliterature, which it would be foolish for an outsider to attempt to summarize. What I want to do is examine what has been made of the case by two of the most theoretically sophisticated commentators so far, the anthropologist Veena Das and the political theorist Partha Chatterjee, and having summarized their *theoretical* reading of the current state of 'actually existing pluralism' in India, compare it with the empirical dissolution of a sociologically naïve notion of the minority 'community' in recent ethnographic accounts by Peter van der Veer and Thomas Hansen.

First, though, we should clarify what the case might be thought to have been 'about'. Patricia Jeffery points out that neither the legal decision in the Shah Bano case, nor the subsequent amendment to the law, had much practical impact on the lives of women in the part of eastern Uttar Pradesh where she has carried out her field research for many years. The bald facts of gender inequality and women's very limited access to property rights cross-cut the division between 'communities'. Jeffery's point is the very valuable one that activists concerned with gender issues should not assume that legal decisions at a national level necessarily have much bearing on the circumstances of everyday life at a local level. But it also, I think, raises another important possibility: that the two communities in eastern Utar Pradesh share rather more in terms of patterns of economic and social relations than their politico-religious leaders would care to acknowledge (Jeffery 2001). If this is the case, and if this evidence is reproduced elsewhere, our reading of the Shah Bano case already has to let go of the more Rawlsian reading – in which different communities have incommensurable ideas of the good and desirable life, and the theoretical problem of seeking a consensus in the absence of shared assumptions (a common culture) becomes *the* political problem in postcolonial India – and shift into a slightly more Taylorian mode. In this perspective, what is at stake is less the practical effect of the court decision in households across India, but more what the court's decision 'says' about the position of minorities in India. In Taylor's terms what is at issue is 'recognition', and in India (unlike Sri Lanka) courts have been central arenas for working through the shifting positions of communities vis-à-vis the postcolonial state.

This possibility is implicitly recognized early in Das' argument in her important essay 'Communities as Political Actors' (Das 1995a). She points out that the wording of the judgement itself, especially the judge's linking of issues of gender equality, minority recognition, and the desirability for uniform legal provision within the nation-state, made the case especially resonant as a 'signifier of issues which touched on several dimensions' (Das 1995a: 95). One of the great strengths of Das' essay is the quizzical way in which she explores these different dimensions, usually starting from this stance of treating the case as a complex signifier. Yet, having begun by acknowledging the 'heterogeneity' of the issues involved – in 1970s anthropological language, the case's symbolic multivocality – at one point Das seems to end up with an argument which seeks out the (single) 'real issue'. This is, she says, 'a question of whether powers of the state should be extended to encroach into the sphere of the family' (Das 1995a: 104). But, rather than trapping her argument in a naïve state–society dichotomy, Das herself is keen to acknowledge the reality of the domestic as a 'site of conflict' and to find ways of addressing women's struggles within that zone without 'subsuming them under the master symbols of state and community' (Das 1995a: 105).

The theoretical problems in a strong state–society distinction become clearer in Partha Chatterjee's contribution to this debate. Chatterjee's piece is an oddly compelling hybrid – an essay which is by his own account about India and its specific problems, but which nevertheless drifts between the specifics of Indian legal and constitutional history and an infinitely more general level of theorizing about governmentality and the state. It is also an essay which ends up focusing very tightly on the issues raised by the Shah Bano case, without once invoking that name or that case itself. Instead, the final argument is about the political possibilities open to a member (female) of an unnamed minority group. Chatterjee's premise in this argument is very similar to Das' identification of the 'real issue'. What is at stake here is the relationship between 'community', for Chatterjee the socio-political entity which liberalism cannot acknowledge, and the state. In particular, the issue is the limits of governmentality in India:

[B]y resisting, on the one hand, the normalizing attempt of the national state to define, classify, and fix the identity of minorities on their behalf . . . and demanding, on the other, that regulative powers within the community be established on a more democratic and internally representative basis, our protagonist will try to engage in a strategic politics that is neither integrationist nor separatist. She will in fact locate herself precisely at the cusp where she can face, on the one side, the assimilationist powers of governmental technology and resist, on the grounds of autonomy and self-representation, its universalist idea of citizenship and, on the other side, struggle, once again on the grounds of autonomy and self-representation, for the emergence of more representative public institutions and practices within her community. (Chatterjee 1995: 37)

Chatterjee's argument depends on a somewhat uncritical transfer of Foucault's sweeping characterization of modern power from Europe to India, with one important proviso: India, implicitly, is somewhere 'where the sway of governmental power is far from general' (Chatterjee 1995), and the 'community' remains a possible locus of resistance to the state.

Of course, Chatterjee could hardly fail to have noticed the argument that 'communities', or at least those communities involved in 'communalism', are themselves products of the classificatory activities of the colonial and postcolonial state (Pandey 1990). Chatterjee is unembarrassed by this problem:

What is problematic here is not so much the existence of bounded categories of population, which the classificatory devices of modern governmental technologies will inevitably impose, but rather the inability of people to negotiate, through a continuous and democratic process of self-representation, the actual content of those categories. That is the new politics that one must try to initiate within the old forms of the modern state. (Chatterjee 1995: 37)

Cynics will, of course, notice how much Chatterjee's 'new politics' owes to the political sociology of American multiculturalism: it is predicated upon that world of more-or-less clearly bounded moral-cultural bubbles I criticized at the start of this chapter. Even non-cynics will be puzzled as to how 'bounded categories' which are imposed by the state should yet be sufficiently free of governmentality that they become prime sites of resistance to the state. It is true that Chatterjee takes on the Orientalist origin of the notion of 'community' elsewhere, in the closing pages of his *The Nation and its Fragments*, but that argument starts at a point of some subtlety – Kaviraj's (1992) delineation of the 'fuzziness' of early modern communities in India – but concludes at a point which is rather more sentimental, the 'narrative of community', 'persistent in its invocation of the rhetoric of love and kinship against the homogenizing sway of the normalized individual' (Chatterjee 1993).

Chatterjee's implicit account of actually existing pluralism, at least as it exists in the religious sphere, is not based on evidence of the actions, institutions, or practices of actual communities. One possible line of critique, anticipated by Das in her paper, would be to query the idea of 'reified cultural communities' and instead address 'questions about the heterogeneity of the community and the multiplicity of identities' (Das 1995a: 112). So, for example, Peter van der Veer's (1992) account of Sufi practice in Surat brings out the internal divisions *within* the category of 'Muslims', between, for example, the reformers of the Tabligh-i-Jamaat who oppose some of the practices and interpretations of the Sufis, and the family and followers of the Sufi *pir*. Some of van der Veer's evidence suggests that Muslims themselves could be plausibly presented as 'profoundly divided by reasonable though incompatible religious, philosophical, and moral doctrines', to borrow Rawls' phrasing. What is especially surprising is how little explicit reference is made in their internal arguments to the presence or absence of the contaminating figure of the Hindu 'other'. Perhaps even more surprising to those unfamiliar with South Asian Islam (but easily impressed by the hysteria around 'fundamentalism') is the profoundly anti-political stance taken by the Tablighis, who see engagement with Indian politics and the Indian state as inherently corrupting.

This sort of example, of the deep differences of moral theory and practice *within* a supposedly unitary 'community', provides a suitable counterpart to Baumann's tracing of the emergence of shared practices and understandings between members of supposedly bounded communities in London. It does not, though, provide decisive empirical refutation to Chatterjee's model of the community and the state. Indeed Chatterjee could claim that internal argument merely confirms his case for recognizing the place of democratic disagreement inside the community, while the Tablighis' hostility to the state similarly accords with his hypothetical minority, whose representatives claim the right not to have to justify their practices in a wider public arena.

In this respect, Hansen's ethnographic contribution to this debate is far more decisive. In the conclusion of an excellent account of what he calls the 'predicaments of secularism' for Mumbai Muslims, Hansen points out that 'meanings of secularism in India are not negotiated between reified cultural communities with fully formed notions of morality and public ethics and a state driven by "reason", but in much less orderly forms' (Hansen 2000: 269). He describes Muslims in 1990s Mumbai as torn between two strategies, whose genealogy goes back to the colonial period and the Gandhian valorization of culture over politics. So one strategy is a project of internal purification and withdrawal from the political, as exemplified at one extreme by the Tabligh-i-Jamaat with its appeal to middle-class Muslims, but also found in different formulations in many other activist groups. Working against this is what he describes as 'a more pragmatic strategy of "plebeian assertion"' (Hansen 2000: 261). One aspect of this is the working-class attempt at embourgoeoisement through investment in education and aspirations to better employment. Another, though, is the engagement in a wider political world through a more assertive, and distinctively plebeian, style of Muslim politics. Although Hansen himself does not make this argument, it is possible to suggest that in this new style of Muslim politics, the stereotypical local 'boss' – that well-known criminal-political hybrid in urban India – provides an image of convergence for members of different communities in Mumbai, just as the idiom of cousin-talk does for young Southallians. Out of these processes we may expect some future fragmentation of any notion of a singular Muslim identity, as well as the emergence of new spaces – unauthorized by the cultural authorities, as it were – within which to imagine being a Muslim. Here then, we have a fairly nuanced account of what I earlier called 'pluralizing strategies' – found in the new style of urban politics – as well as the constant work of counter-pluralism, found in the Tabligh, and all the other organizations concerned to resist the moral decay that is thought to come through direct political engagement with the state.

My allusion to hybrids brings a comparison to mind. Hansen's depiction of the twin operations of purification within the community, and networking and alliance building to the outside, carries a – presumably unconscious – echo of the language of Bruno Latour's *We Have Never Been Modern* (Latour 1993). Starting from his own work within the sociology of science, Latour argues that the cultural work of modernity involves the establishment of a number of impossible but necessary dichotomies – between tradition and modernity, nature and culture, scientific reason and political interest. In practice, networks cut across the divide between science and politics, hybrids confound the distinction between nature and culture, and much of our time is spent on the work of purification, suppressing the links which are not supposed to exist between domains which should stay completely separate (cf. Spencer 2003). Here we have another way to think about the impossibility of keeping cultural 'things' apart from each other – Leach's shocking truism that 'human beings in adjacent areas of the map are likely to have relations with one another' – while also admitting the huge effort we put into trying to pretend that this is not the case. And, lest we forget, Latour's way forward is based on what he calls a symmetrical anthropology of the modern world with a strong commitment to ethnographic holism – to following our noses as we trace people's social relations to wherever they lead us.

Pluralism and the Political

Let me draw some obvious parallels with what we know about the fate of pluralism in Sri Lanka. The Sri Lankan state, it would be generally conceded, has not dealt with the issue of pluralism especially well in its postcolonial politics. Since the 1950s the two largest 'communities', Sinhala and Tamil, have drifted further apart; since the mid-1980s the country has been in a state of civil war. Yet the issues that have separated the communities have not, on the whole, been what we might call Rawlsian issues – deeply incompatible notions of the public good; nor have they been contested in the arena of the courts, over issues of collective and individual, universal and minority, rights. Mostly they have been issues of recognition and respect, of access to relatively scarce public goods like university education and state employment in the early years of the schism, and of freedom from military repression and the threat of official violence since the late 1970s. It is true that in recent years, as the Colombo government became increasingly aware of the impossibility of imposing a military solution, something like a problem of incommensurability has emerged. But that incommensurability lies not between 'Sinhalas' and 'Tamils' *tout court*, but between their respective political representatives, the governments of the UNP and the People's Alliance on the Sinhala side, and, in the Tamil case, the leadership of the Liberation Tigers of Tamil Ealam.

It is worth pausing at this point to remind ourselves of some of the things the Sri Lankan conflict is *not* about. It is not, for example, about the contradictions of legal pluralism. Sri Lankan courts recognize a remarkable jumble of different legal codes yet, for whatever reason, this situation has never been much of a political issue. There has been occasional grumbling about the difficulty of outsiders buying property on the Jaffna peninsula, or rumours of Sinhala businessmen making sudden conversions to Islam in order to offload unwanted spouses at low cost, but these have hardly been central to the developing conflict. Indeed, I have been unable to find any mention of the diversity of personal law, either in the vast academic literature on the Sri Lankan conflict, or in the specific devolution proposals put forward by the successive governments since the 1990s.

This is not all that is missing in the academic literature. For all the invocations of words like 'ethnic' and 'ethnicity' there is, in Sri Lanka, almost no published ethnography of what we might call the everyday work of ethnicity: the working through of issues of similarity and difference in work and the economy, kinship, or religious practice.[1] When anthropologists like myself have talked of the 'ethnic problem' in Sri Lanka we have almost always talked from a perspective within one of the taken-for-granted divisions of the population – usually Sinhala or Tamil. Because of this empirical weakness, we are some way short of providing the kind

[1] There are exceptions, most notably among the senior generation of ethnographers who have worked in the island, like Denis McGilvray (1982; 1998), who has struggled for many years to deal with the diversity of the mixed Muslim and Tamil areas of the east coast, Jock Stirrat (1984; 1992), whose work on Catholicism is especially sensitive to shifting emphases in people's chosen self-identifications in terms of religious affiliation or linguistic community, as well as James Brow (1978; 1996) on Vedda identity (but not 'Vedda culture'), and Charles Kemp (1984) on the dense political-economic ties between Sinhala and Tamil in and around the tea estates.

of coherent description of local diversity in practice we find in the work of Baumann or Hansen. And we are especially unable to investigate how the big schism of the war is refracted by the many other differences – of class and education, language, caste, religion – which either cut across or reinforce the ethnic divide. Twenty years on, anthropologists have hardly started to understand how Sri Lanka works (and doesn't work) as a plural society.

I started this chapter by suggesting that discrete cultures are not the givens of human social life, but, in so far as they exist at all, are the fragile and strictly temporary products of a great deal of human effort, much of which we could broadly label 'political'. The work of purification, to borrow Latour's phrase again, and the counter-work of pluralization take place in specific historical and political-economic circumstances. That deadly chimera we call the state can appear on the side of purification and on the side of pluralization. In Hansen's Mumbai, political engagement offers new possibilities for the collective imaginary, while political withdrawal is, for many, an attempt at closure. In Colombo, where the argument in this chapter was first presented, the price of political engagement in recent decades has often been terrible. Yet a glance at the world around us, in all its manifold complexity, suggests that those who would insist on closure, and who would silence all alternative possibilities – in the name of the nation, the community, or the state, and by violence if they deem it necessary – are unlikely to succeed.

Politics as Counter-pluralism

In theory, anthropology has much to offer in public debate about pluralism. The relational version of ethnic identity, put forward by Leach, Barth, and others in the 1950s and 1960s (Barth 1969), has been successfully revived in recent work like Baumann's on Southall, but it has a much more muted presence in broader argument about politics and culture. Anthropologists writing on ethnic violence, as I started to suggest in the previous chapter, have been too often dazzled by the moment of violence itself, producing a decontextualized version of the world in which violence occurs. One component of that missing context, in some accounts at least, is the area of life I have called 'the political'. But another, equally important, component is the world of everyday pluralism: all those situations and settings in which people, averagely imperfect as they are, manage to get by with one another. This is the zone of accommodation, the place where no one is required to love their neighbour – indeed they are allowed to fear or even hate that person – but neither is anyone expected to attack or kill their neighbour.

Consider one of the most moving recent anthropological contributions to public understanding of this kind of accommodation. On the screen, a woman is talking: 'It's the same as before as far as neighbours are concerned.' In the background there is a faint sound of shells exploding. The woman is a Bosnian Muslim in a village about two hours' drive from Sarajevo where the shells are falling. It is early 1993 and the village has a mixed population of two-thirds Muslims and one third Catholics. An old Muslim lady visits her best friend, a Catholic. 'Whatever happens', she says, 'we'll drink coffee together.'

These are moments from the opening scenes of a remarkable film called *We Are All Neighbours* directed by Debbie Christie in collaboration with the anthropologist Tone Bringa.[2] I close this chapter with these scenes because the film, it seems to me, can serve as an exemplar of the kinds of quiet illumination anthropology can offer in situations like the war in former Yugoslavia. The film documents the disintegration of an 'ethnically' mixed community as the war moves closer and closer. Mutual confidence in ties of friendship and neighbourliness, eloquently asserted on both sides at the start of the film, ebbs away as the film progresses. The Croatian Defence Force sets up rocket-launchers 4 kilometres away,

---

[2] *We Are All Neighbours*, directed by Debbie Christie in collaboration with Tone Bringa, Granada, 55 minutes.

aimed, so the Muslims believe, at Muslim houses; someone says, rather more desperately this time, 'We are all neighbours and we'll have to live together afterwards.' A Croatian gun emplacement appears on a hill overlooking the village and the relations between neighbours get more strained: 'We're barely greeting each other, saying "Good day".' One of the old ladies who shared coffee with her neighbour at the start spots her friend across a field and cajoles her to join her with the film crew: 'Come out into the light.' The tiny figure in the distance refuses to budge. 'How can everything change?' the anthropologist asks one of the villagers after the guns have appeared on the hill; 'It changed' is the simple reply.

It changed. The impersonality of the phrase is telling. What the film shows – perhaps better than any source I can think of – is the way in which violence of a certain sort remakes everyday relationships, corroding old friendships, apparently compelling unwilling people to take sides in a conflict they have already said they want no part of. As friends cease to visit each other's houses, the responsibility seems to lie elsewhere – especially in the gun emplacements, the impersonal technology of warfare taking the blame for the failure of human agents to arrest the divisions in the village. The message the viewer takes from one reading of the film is this: 'We never wanted these things to happen, and, if we'd been left alone, they never would have happened.' To this, though, must be added the further message, stated after the violence finally touched the village itself: 'Her neighbour told her, "I killed your husband." There can be no more living together.'

We Are All Neighbours is a very unusual war film. There are no shots of fighting, only undramatic footage of the ill-equipped Bosnian militia sharing cigarettes and shivering in the cold night, and no bodies, except for a dead horse lying on its side in a field after the Muslim houses in the village have been burned and looted. It is, instead, a domestic film, concerned with kitchens and cooking, and the ways in which kinship and friendship are expressed through shared food and drink. In the final scenes, earlier footage of domestic activity is juxtaposed with shots of the same houses, burned out and deserted. Domesticity, it becomes clear, is a matter of gender, and in the early scenes women of both communities reflect on the burdens they have to carry while the men go about their masculine business.

Rather than melodramatic reportage from the frontline, we desperately need better, and more politically sophisticated, analyses of the kind of rough-and-ready civility shown so vividly in Bringa's film. We also need to pay more attention to the processes that reduce the possibilities for civil co-existence. The arrival of a gun battery is an extreme case, but there are other ways of producing the same effect: an election dominated by populist rhetoric aimed at the outsider, the refugee, or the asylum-seeker; officially sanctioned moral panics, propagated on the radio or through the press, which then 'take off' in an atmosphere of fear and rumour; or even the introduction of constitutional arrangements, predicated on a 'pluralistic' model of a multicultural society, which then force people to act as if there really are walls around their 'culture'.

There is one final task, which is if anything more important still, but also quite a bit more difficult, especially for academic anthropologists unused to thinking prospectively about the consequences of policy choices. That task is to think creatively about the ways in which new political arrangements might build upon, and thereby 'scale up', those areas of rough-and-ready civility which I have called the zone of everyday pluralism. This is difficult work, with little opportunity for satisfyingly simple moral gestures, and absolutely no guaranteed audience for any proposals we might come up with.

EIGHT

Politics and Counter-politics

Batticaloa, February 2006

To a casual visitor, if such can be imagined, the town of Batticaloa on the eastern coast of Sri Lanka seems remarkably unscathed by its recent history. Children walk to school in their immaculately white shirts, clusters of cyclists clog the bridges, prawn fishermen drift in their canoes on the lagoon that encircles the town. There are, it is true, army checkpoints on the road, and the anarchic local traffic frequently parts to let through a white 4×4, be-flagged avatar of the international humanitarian community, its occupants in their air-conditioned seats staring out at the humanity they are here to serve. Each jeep sports a flag to identify the INGO they adhere to. Some, like those of the Norwegian-administered International Monitoring Mission, are here because this is supposed to be a post-conflict zone. Rather more are in the business of post-Tsunami aid and reconstruction.

The Tsunami in December 2004 hit this coastline hard. The town itself was protected by its lagoons, but whole villages along the beach close by were flattened and, fifteen months on, the rebuilding of permanent homes has hardly begun. The stalled rebuilding process is a complex story. A national agreement between the government and the LTTE for joint mechanisms for the distribution of aid, painstakingly negotiated

5 The work of counter-politics (Batticaloa, 2006)

under the watchful eye of the big donors, was kicked into touch by the courts on constitutional grounds before it ever really took hold. But even without this setback, there are other reasons for the slow response: local government structures have been weakened by years of political interference, and even more by years of war. Local political patronage can be enough to launch local projects, but it cannot generate regional planning infrastructures, or co-ordinated housing programmes. The big international agencies have at times been fighting over projects they can show to their supporters back home: a field of unused boats by the road into town bears witness to the consequences – bright red and white, fibre-glass, they are, as their signboard proclaims, the gift of a big NGO. All they lack are appropriate recipients. There are further constraints. The coast south of the town was especially densely populated, and the government's proposed ban on new building within 100 metres of the shoreline has left would-be redevelopers with no place to go. And then there is land. Twenty years of conflict, twenty years of endless rearrangements of population, has left a trail of land disputes up and down the coast. Before you build you need to know whose land you are building on, and often there is no easy answer to that apparently easy question.

I am in Batticaloa for two reasons. A Ph.D. student has been living here for the last year, and I am eager to learn from her about 'the situation' (as everyone refers to it). I have also got involved with an attempt to rebuild the research capacity of the local universities. A University was started here just before the war took hold of the east. Somehow it has survived two decades of war, but not without cost. In the mid-1990s the Muslim students and staff left to found a new University thirty miles to the south, complaining that the activities of the LTTE made it impossible for them to continue here. My colleagues are now working to reverse this process, by bringing three universities together in a consortium for research and training. Not least of the attractions is the explicit ambition to 'de-ethnicize' this corner of the educational system.

Out on the campus I get a better sense of what people are referring to when they invoke 'the situation'. After two years of ceasefire, internal tensions within the LTTE finally came to a head in March 2004. The eastern leadership announced a split from the northern commanders: for years the east had supplied the foot soldiers for the struggle, many of them children forcibly recruited from poor villages in this area, but the movement itself was dominated by a small group of leaders from the north. The northern leadership initially insisted the split was a purely internal affair, and moved its fighters in to reassert territorial control around Batticaloa. The result has been less than successful. The LTTE control areas north and west of the town itself. But the breakaway group has its own bases elsewhere to the west, and under the benign gaze of government security forces, have been conducting their own campaign of assassination and abduction. The LTTE has responded with killings of its own. Most recently it has raised the stakes by targeting government troops. A couple of weeks before I arrive, four people had been killed when an army truck and a bus full of police and soldiers were blown up in the centre of the town. Further south, a separate conflict has emerged, this time between between the LTTE and a powerful Muslim politician. Again there are murders and counter-murders, threats and disappearances.

Here is just one story I was told. The University is in the border zone, just a few miles from the main areas of LTTE control in this part of the country. A few months after the split, the bodies of seven members of the breakaway group were discovered in a house in a Colombo suburb. It was generally assumed they had been killed by the LTTE. One of the dead was a young man well known to many people on the campus. A local boy whose mother still lived nearby, he had been a bright and popular student before going off to join the LTTE some years earlier. When the split came, he sided with the eastern group under their leader 'Colonel Karuna'. Although his body was brought home for the funeral, word quickly spread that anyone who attended it would put themselves at risk. The family was instructed to take down the funeral decorations from the house. After much anguish, only a handful of his former friends and teachers felt able to go. Hearing this story, told to me only eighteen months after the funeral, I was struck again by the way in which violence and fear were explicitly directed at key threads in the social fabric. A funeral in Sri Lanka is pre-eminently an occasion for making evident, and reaffirming, the social networks in which a person is embedded. The denial of a full funeral is tantamount to the denial of full personhood. And the attempt to undermine 'normal' markers of sociality through the warnings to stay clear of the funeral further corroded everyday expectations of trust, friendship, and collegiality on the campus. This was what the slogan 'no war – no peace', coined to describe the continuing low-level violence after the formal ceasefire, meant in people's everyday life.

A couple of days earlier I had had a conversation with a long-time peace activist in the town. I was trying to explain why I felt that the ceasefire, for all its flaws and failings, still marked a step forward in the long route out of the conflict. Attitudes had changed in the south, I insisted; the main political parties felt obliged to pay lip-service to the cause of peace even if they continued to exploit the fears aroused by the ethnic other for their short-tem political gain. 'I don't know about all this', my companion responded, 'Perhaps we are too close to things that happen here everyday. Perhaps we don't pay enough attention to all the politics.'

Then on the last day of the visit, I was back with the same peace activist. A small ceremony had been arranged for the families of three recent victims of the violence – one shot by the security forces, one shot by the LTTE, one who had disappeared months before and whose murdered body had lain in the city mortuary unclaimed for weeks. The ceremony was a tree-planting to mark the victims' death and support those families who were unable, because of 'the situation', to mourn in public. It is being held in the living room of a house shared by an NGO and a group of feminist activists, some of whom have been swimming against the inexorable currents of 'the situation' since the first serious violence in the early 1980s. As well as the families of the victims, there are guests from local NGOs, and a couple of visiting researchers. Pictures of the victims are set up in the middle of the room, and oil lamps lit in front of them. Someone explains in Tamil, and then again in English for the benefit of the outsiders, why we are here, why it is important, for the families but also for everyone, to mark the loss of these people, how in death they are, like us, human beings first and foremost.

When I get back to Colombo a few days later I describe the scene to a friend, another long-time feminist peace activist who knows the

Batticaloa group well. There are those, she tells me, who object to this kind of activity because it is too personal, because it depoliticizes 'the situation'. She is not one of them, she hastens to add, but she thinks it important I should be aware of this more critical reading of an event that I had clearly found deeply moving.

Counter-politics

What does it mean to 'depoliticize' victimhood? Why did my interlocutor say 'Perhaps we don't pay enough attention to all the politics'? In a curious way, I felt the questions raised by this moment returned me to the central theme of this book.

If the political really is reducible, in Schmitt's (1996 [1932]: 26) terms, to the difference between friend and enemy, then the landscape of agonistic violence I found around Batticaloa is pre-eminently political. It resonates with the picture so memorably evoked by Brass in Uttar Pradesh (chapter six): this is not a situation in which we can easily separate the state from other forces at work, it is a situation in which 'law and order' is at best a half-forgotten promise for most people. The forces are multiple, their alignments shifting and unstable. Violence is central to much that we might call political, but each actor works with a different repertoire and each act of violence might carry a different implicit meaning. So, for example, the LTTE, for long the masters of what Benjamin (Benjamin 1979 [1920/1]) called 'law-making' violence, have since 2002 been concerned to present themselves as a more sober and self-evidently state-like entity, with courts and police and human rights' commissions. Out here in the east, though, their erstwhile cadres have been deploying a cruder politics of fear, picking off those who continue to identify themselves with the northern leadership. The response has been muddled. Reprisal attacks on troops and police have not been officially sponsored, the LTTE insist, they are spontaneous acts of 'the people', a Lankan *intifada* beyond their control. So, according to one informant, the LTTE in another town in the region handed out hand grenades to any member of 'the people' who cared to take them. But, because they were handing out hand grenades in a state-like way, the recipients were asked to sign for them. Meanwhile the feud with the Muslim politician and his supporters employs violence in a slightly different political idiom. The villages on the edge of the LTTE areas are some of the poorest in the region and have long suffered coercive child recruitment by the paramilitaries. In this latest phase of post-conflict conflict, they are under pressure from all sides: public identification with one group invites attack by the other; non-identification invites attack by both. There would seem to be no escape.

'The situation' is also potentially intelligible in the language of sovereignty, as I employed it in chapter six. In the villages on the edge of control, different groups appear and demand some sign of allegiance, threatening those aligned with their enemies with death. The villagers, caught in this impossible impasse, are reduced to something very much like Agamben's 'bare life' (Agamben 1998). Lacking the instrumental means to control 'the state', or what is left of the state apparatus, here the different players assert their claims to sovereignty through the idiom of death. This zone of fear and abjection is not a zone of 'state failure' or 'state withdrawal'. If anything there is too much state-like conduct, too much assertion of sovereignty by the taking of bare life. That politics of performative agonism I encountered a quarter-century earlier in my village ethnography is here taken to its purest form: ideology has been all but forgotten, even the encompassing fictions of the nation have fragmented back into warring factions.

This is not a land beyond politics; it is a land suffused with too much politics. And the activists I met who conducted the modest ceremony of memorialization were clearly well aware of that. These were hardly naïve innocents. Some had worked alongside Rajani Thiranagama before her murder in Jaffna in 1989. Others had been here in Batticaloa, not so silent witnesses, through some of the darkest years of the war. They knew the micro-politics of the situation as intimately as anyone, and every move they made, every gesture of hope or love or defiance, was carefully calibrated to fit the known room for manouevre in an ever unstable situation. Theirs was a performance of the counter-political, a self-conscious attempt to resist the logic of division that seeped through every encounter in the region. If the decay of everyday sociality, so vividly recorded in Bringa and Christie's Bosnian film, poses a question to all politically alert anthropologists, then these activists are struggling towards an answer. Their case and their work allows me to open up the conclusion of this book to a whole world of new questions and new connections.

Politics, Anti-politics, Counter-politics

One first set of questions returns us to the theme of the political. A key move in classical political anthropology was to redefine the scope of the political, first by exploring political functions rather than political institutions (what mechanisms maintain order and stability in the absence of a central state?), and secondly by stressing political behaviour, political process, or political performance (how do actors compete for resources, pursue strategies, jostle for power?). The first move was consolidated in British Africanist work of the 1930s and 1940s (Fortes and Evans-Pritchard 1940), the second pursued in the early work of Edmund Leach, and in the circle around Max Gluckman in Manchester (Leach 1954; Turner 1957; Bailey 1969). Each move produces a distinctive set of unresolvable problems.

The first set of problems derives from the artificial attempt to identify politics 'without' the state. The functionalist concern with the sources of social order, it has recently been argued, at once erased the presence of the colonial power as a political condition of possibility for so-called 'stateless societies' in the present, yet was all the while 'haunted' by assumptions and language derived from the understanding of the modern European state (Das and Poole 2004). Either a certain political philosophy of the state was smuggled back in to anthropological analysis as an unacknowledged norm: order is a problem, violence must be contained, and so on. Or, as in other, more recent, work informed by critical approaches to the state, the world is re-imagined in terms of spaces inside and outside the state, the zone of dominance and the space of resistance, the modern and the cultural: a social topography which reproduces the very mystification it might be expected to challenge.

In chapter two I traced the consequences of this move in the work of some leading Subaltern theorists, and pointed out the paradox that arguments which celebrated the impervious boundary between the modern state and authentic politics in India were being advanced in a period of unprecedented engagement with modern electoral politics, in which previously marginal groups in Indian society – Dalits for example – increasingly turned to the repertoire of representative democracy in order to advance their claims for recognition and respect (Corbridge and Harriss 2000). The consequences of these moves were neither trivial, nor in any sense self-evident. Poor people did not simply commit their fate to elected politicians in a spirit of deluded mystification, on the one hand; but neither did the electoral success of low-caste politicians sweep away the detritus of centuries of injustice. Most obviously, there is no evidence that the apparent success of liberal political institutions is producing a subcontinent peopled with copy-book liberal political subjects. The effects of the political, like the world itself, are rather more complex than that. A low-caste leader like Laloo Prasad (chapter two) not only challenges any sense of what is politically possible: his actions and gestures must somehow also impact on people's everyday sense of what might be socially possible. In short, the fertility of the political pushes at the limits of the social imagination.

The second problem with the inherited language of 'political anthropology', as it was conceived and practised in the 1940s and 1950s, is its indifference to the moral evaluation of political action. The language of 'political behaviour', so popular among the political scientists of the 1950s and 1960s, is a homogenizing language. Its hidden twin is the rich demotic domain of 'anti-politics', which can variously invoke 'religion', 'community', 'family', or 'nation' as the necessary antithesis to the political (cf. Hansen 1999: 229). Politics and anti-politics, the agonistic and the altruistic, individual interest and collective morality: seen from far enough away, these are only *rhetorical* alternatives, contained *within* the field of the political. In truth, there is no 'outside' outside politics, no safe space from which to mount a critique which is not itself a part of that which is being criticized. 'Anti-politics' is itself a product of the political. At the level of rhetoric and symbolism the political and the anti-political are symbiotically connected, as new politicians claim to transcend the petty squabbles of agonistic politics even as they enter into the same squabbles. As the new claims fade back into the background of 'normal' politics, they leave behind them their own additions to local repertoires of power.

I think, though, that the activists in Batticaloa are not best thought of as exponents of this kind of anti-politics. Their activities are consciously crafted to defuse the effects of the political: as such, I would prefer to describe them as 'counter-political' rather than 'anti-political'. Whereas the anti-political is rooted in a paradox – the exploitation, for *political* purposes, of popular unease with the moral implications of actually existing politics – the counter-political aspires to avoid the divisive heart of the political altogether. As such, as I shall argue, it offers an interesting model for future anthropological practice.

The Political and the Past

First, though, I should return to one theme that has haunted much of this book: what Ghosh (chapter three) called 'the irreversible triumph of the language that had usurped all the others', the language of political modernity. My argument has struggled throughout against a version of the postcolonial world in which 'Western' political institutions, or 'Western' political languages, are simply imposed upon other idioms and structures, and in which the imbalance of power between colonizer and

colonized gives the new institutions and languages the sense of inexora-
bility that Ghosh describes in his lament. This view, I have suggested, is
part of a widespread structure of feeling encountered on the academic left,
a rich mélange of pessimism and critique, at once founded in, yet critical
of, the simple moral and political binaries of late colonial nationalism.

I will return to the moral landscape of postcolonial critique in the
next section, but here I want to focus on the political assumptions that
shape much of the critique. Probably the single most problematic aspect
of these is the epochal view of history and change that informs it. This
is not merely a world of 'before' and 'after', it is a world in which our
understanding of 'after' is predicated upon a contrastive construction of
'before' as all the things the present lacks. The present lacks 'tradition',
or 'culture', or 'authenticity' or 'enchantment'. As these examples suggest,
there is nothing especially new in this position – it is the very stuff of
the nineteenth- and early twentieth-century romantic critique of industrial society, of thinkers like Ruskin who so influenced the young Gandhi
(Hansen 1997). It is also at the heart of Weber's pessimistic apprehension
of the modern. And the architecture of 'before' and 'after', the great rup-
ture that heralds the birth of the modern, animates Foucault's great early
works on madness and the birth of the human sciences (Foucault 1967
[1961]; Foucault 1974 [1966]). Foucault's genealogical critique offers considerable critical purchase on the assumptions and institutional structure
of the present, concerned as it is to show the contingent, non-necessary
status of contemporary institutions and practices. But the intellectual
dangers are twofold. One is the trap of anachronism, of implicitly sort-
ing the world into two different, incommensurable time-frames. On the
other hand, a more or less purely theoretical apprehension of 'modern'
political institutions, which in the end is what Foucault's own work offers,
however critical its spirit, is a poor guide to the much weirder world of
actually existing politics.

When I first struggled to interpret the politics of early 1980s Sri Lanka
I started with a straightforward act of rebellion against the temporal

assumptions other analysts had worked with (Spencer 1990b). Whereas the received wisdom treated Sinhala nationalism, and Sinhala–Tamil antagonism, as self-evidently ancient, I instead asked how people's sense of who they were, and how it mattered, had been changed by the effects of modern mass politics. But the workings of party politics at village level, the everyday antagonisms of modern mass politics, did not, *pace* the received wisdom, strike me as a self-evidently 'new' phenomenon at all. In the nineteenth century, peasants had used – or attempted to use – the machinery of the colonial state to pursue 'private' disputes with their neighbours; in the late twentieth century they used party affiliations and the carnivalesque world of the political. Antagonism was not a product of modern party politics, but the theatre of electoral representation described in chapter three did provide new repertoires, with new implications, for the public expression of antagonism. Clearly things had changed – democratic political arrangements brought new dangers, and the events in Sri Lanka since 1983 illustrate those dangers clearly enough, in the toxic use, by state and anti-state actors alike, of capillaries of local political antagonism in the insurgency of the late 1980s, and in the state-level ensemble of inclusion and exclusion, friend and foe, order and disorder, employed by both parties in the civil war of the 1990s.

One way to read Schmitt's definition of the political is as a reworking of Hobbes' 'state of Warre': 'Its critical twist was to project the state of nature depicted in Leviathan, the war of all against all in which individual agents are pitted against each other, onto the plane of modern collective conflicts: thereby transforming civil society itself into a second state of nature' (Anderson 2005: 5). The authoritarian political conclusions Schmitt drew from this insight are famously abhorrent, but they should not in themselves disqualify the argument itself. What Schmitt's claim offers is an invitation to reject the pious political myth that 'mature' politics somehow exist in a realm beyond conflict and antagonism, and with it the assumption that a Hobbesian state of Warre was settled at some foundational moment in modern political arrangements, such that its increasingly frequent reappearance in our world can be dismissed as an aberration, an unfortunate anachronism. Perhaps most important of all for the present crisis we face, it suggests that democracy – for all its attractions and excitements – is as likely to serve as a conduit for conflict, not a replacement for it. Important recent work in historical sociology has shown the umbilical cord linking democratic politics to projects of ethnic or nationalist exclusion: the moment when 'the people', in whose name a modern democracy acts, define themselves in opposition to some other kind of 'people', is the moment when we glimpse the deep structure of some of the most horrifying political calamities of our times (Wimmer 2002; Mann 2005). Those calamities are above all political calamities.

The anthropology of the political is, then, the anthropology of 'the political', that compelling but morally unsettling space in which friend is differentiated from foe. It gives us an enduring object, the working of agonism in social life, and a wonderfully rich set of problems to grapple with. In this book the central problem has been the social and cultural effect of certain recent institutional arrangements and modes of political imagination – the state and its ideological avatar, the nation, representative democracy and its manifestation as electoral dramaturgy. How do these changed institutional arrangements affect the scale and dynamic of the political? One key of course is material: the technological capacity for action of modern states, especially for action on their own populations, is potentially greater than before. As are the material respources at stake. I have not dwelt on issues of political economy or distributive justice in this book, not because they are unimportant, but because I wanted to avoid the temptation to subsume the distinctive workings of the political into more familiar, and perhaps more comfortable, materialist language. This is not to deny any role for material interests in my central examples: both the JVP and the LTTE in Sri Lanka are capable of using the language of distributive justice to potent effect. But, as I argued in chapter five, there is an obvious disproportion between their experience of the state as material provider and the sacrifices they are prepared to make for a state of their own. Similarly, the levels of participation and enthusiasm manifest in electoral politics make little sense when we gauge them against the possibility of significant return to the participants. So, in the end, it was not capitalism, globalization, neo-liberalism, or class conflict, still less ethnicity, culture, or religion, that sent Sri Lanka spiralling into civil war in the early 1980s. If it was any one thing, it was the political. There is a tale to be told about the links between political conflict and poverty, for sure, but the links are complex and the causal relations flow both ways. But if I learned one thing from the events I witnessed and pondered on as a fledgling fieldworker in the early 1980s, it was the intellectual bankruptcy of a purely interest-based understanding of the political.

Anthropology as Counter-politics

In the early 1980s, Marilyn Strathern published a sharp analysis of what she saw as the necessary dissonance between anthropology and feminism (Strathern 1987). Despite their superficially congenial relationship, anthropology and feminism were, she argued, at root different kinds of project. Both were oriented to an understanding of 'the Other', but whereas anthropology (as it was in the 1980s) sought to give voice to its Other, by textual experiment or co-operative fieldwork practice, for feminism the Other was patriarchy, a condition to be overcome and destroyed. For anthropology, 'the Other is not under attack. On the contrary, the effort is to create a relation with the Other, as in the search for a medium of expression that will offer mutual interpretation, perhaps visualized as a common text, or a dialogue' (Strathern 1987: 289). For feminism the relation to the Other is antagonistic; for anthropology the relationship aspires to co-operation and dialogue. One wishes to change, the other to understand. At this point in Strathern's staged dialogue, feminism could be said to represent a version of 'the political', in the terms in which I have been exploring it, while anthropological practice is necessarily and inherently counter-political in aspiration. That is one reason for starting this chapter with the peace activists, their domestic ceremony knowingly making a common human ground for hope in a world poisoned by the political. If they are doing anything, they are, in Strathern's terms, striving to 'create a relation'. Strathern's analysis is based on a certain stylized version of both 'anthropology' and 'feminism', and the dissonance she uncovers works itself through as an implication of the contrast she has herself staged. The point is not that the two projects cancel each other out – rather, it is that each rubs the other against the grain, by challenging the axioms upon which they base their intellectual and moral authority. This seems to me a useful model for thinking about anthropology's relationship to the political.

If we step back to the broad-brush world of current polemics, then anthropology is necessarily always aspiring to some sort of counter-political practice. When Huntington and his supporters set out their divisions between 'friend' and 'foe', and locate them at what they cheerfully describe as a 'civilizational' level, anthropology can only object. The objection may be simply empirical: the divisions that Huntington finds so self-evident dissolve into confusion when viewed in closer focus, as I suggested in chapter one. I believe, though, that rather more is at stake. Our objection as anthropologists to the currently popular language of civilizational difference has to be founded on an ethic of suspicion towards *all* political divisions between friend and foe. That is to say, we should refuse to treat any claims to incommensurability and absolute difference – whether expressed in religious, cultural, or political terms – as given aspects of our world. Without such an ethic, our intellectual practice as anthropologists becomes impossible. With an ethic of this sort as a starting point for reflection, our practice gains the possibility of political, as well as intellectual, purchase on the situations in which we engage.

For such an ethic to be fruitful, it can only ever offer a starting point for hard and unsentimental analysis of the situation at hand. There are some obvious traps to avoid. One is the reproduction of the received divisions, but with the values switched round. Since Strathern wrote her piece on feminism in the 1980s, there has been a sea-change in the moral tone of anthropological writing. It is a commonplace that anthropological writing since the 1980s has started to embrace the fluid and uncertain. What is less often commented upon is that this shift has been accompanied by a parallel embrace of political and moral certainties. Starting with the 1980s vogue for resistance studies, anthropologists have been less and less inhibited about wearing their political-ethical hearts on their sleeves. To borrow Lawrence Cohen's astute characterization, much of our work has become informed by a spirit of 'perfomative moralization' (Cohen 1998: xxiii). One has to be careful in phrasing one's criticism here. Like Cohen, I 'appreciate the sentiment' in this work (in all possible senses of the term). In case of confusion, I too am 'against' bad things in our world, whether they be ethnic cleansing, violence against women (and children, and men), poverty, the predations of global capital, or the workings of local political oppression. But the point of an anthropological analysis of any of these topics is not to display my sensibility and my certainties: it is to subject all political certainties to empirical and theoretical scrutiny. When the sociologist Howard Becker stuck his head above the parapet of 1960s value-free social science in a seminal paper called 'Whose Side Are We On?', he was careful to warn against the dangers of sentimentality:

We are sentimental when we refuse, for whatever reason, to investigate some matter that should properly be regarded as problematic. We are sentimental, especially, when our reason is that we would prefer not to know what is going on, if to know would be to violate some sympathy whose existence we may not even be aware of. (Becker 1967: 246)

Becker's warnings against sentimentality echo, of course, Machiavelli's foundational argument for realism in political analysis: 'because I want to write what will be useful to anyone who understands, it seems to me better to concentrate on what really happens' (Machiavelli 1988: 54). The problem with sentimentality is that it clouds understanding.

The case for a *useful* counter-political anthropology cannot, then, rely on appeals to sentiment, to ideas of how we would like the world to be. It has to be firmly realist in aspiration. Yet, that realism is necessarily a situated realism: the landscape of the political is by definition a contested landscape, and there is no external viewpoint which ensures an even view of the territory at stake. So a fieldworker will always have partial knowledge of the political field. But also, any word of any use in our theoretical vocabulary is bound to be an example of what Ian Hacking calls an 'interactive kind' – a category employed by self-aware agents, whose reading of our descriptions could necessarily change the nature of the thing described (Hacking 1999). So, as I pointed out in chapter three, the language of anthropological analysis may also be the language of nationalist argument. We cannot extricate ourselves from the world of the political, and we cannot describe it in a language which is not itself part of that world. Just because there is no epistemological escape from this partial and positioned knowledge, it is all the more important that we treat our own assumptions with all the suspicion we can muster.

In the 1960s and 1970s the study of the political was the scene of a brief skirmish between proponents of scientistic and hermeneutic approaches to the human sciences. In opposition to the prevailing assumptions of political science, philosophers like Alasdair MacIntyre (MacIntyre 1971) and Charles Taylor (Taylor 1985a) argued eloquently for the importance of grounding any comparative study of the political in local interpretations of local meanings. That was an argument which sadly passed most anthropologists by at the time, for reasons I have explored elsewhere (Spencer 1997b). In one of its most memorable moments, Taylor's magisterial essay on 'Interpretation and the Sciences of Man' ends with the following plea:

These [hermeneutical sciences of man] cannot be *wertfrei* [value-free]; they are moral sciences in a more radical sense than the eighteenth century understood . . [T]heir successful prosecution requires a high degree of self-knowledge, a freedom from illusion, in the sense of error which is rooted and expressed in one's way of life; for our incapacity to understand is rooted in our own self-definitions, hence in what we are. (Taylor 1985a [1971]: 57)

A moral science rooted in self-knowledge and systematic questioning of our own self-definitions: three decades on, I cannot think of a better agenda for a reborn anthropology of the political.

Bibliography

Abrams, P. 1988 [1977]. 'Notes on the Difficulty of Studying the State', *Journal of Historical Sociology* 1: 58–89.

Abu-Lughod, L. 1990. 'The Romance of Resistance: Tracing Transformations of Power through Bedouin Women', *American Ethnologist* 17: 41–55.

——— 1991. 'Writing against Culture', in *Recapturing Anthropology: Working in the Present*, ed. R. Fox. Santa Fe, NM: School of American Research Press.

Adams, V. 1996. *Tigers of the Snow and Other Virtual Sherpas: An Ethnography of Himalayan Encounters*. Princeton, NJ: Princeton University Press.

——— 1998. *Doctors for Democracy: Health Professionals in the Nepal Revolution*. Cambridge: Cambridge University Press.

Agamben, G. 1998. *Homo Sacer: Sovereign Power and Bare Life*. Stanford, CA: Stanford University Press.

Alexander, P. 1995. *Sri Lankan Fishermen: Rural Capitalism and Peasant Society*, 2nd edn. *Asian Studies Association of Australia South Asian Publications Series 9*. Delhi: Sterling.

Alter, J. S. 1993. 'The Body of One Color: Indian Wrestling, the Indian State, and Utopian Somatics', *Cultural Anthropology* 8: 49–72.

Amin, S. 1984. 'Gandhi as Mahatma: Gorakhpur District, Eastern UP, 1921–2', in *Subaltern Studies III*, ed. R. Guha. Delhi: Oxford University Press.

Anderson, B. 1983. *Imagined Communities: Reflections on the Origin and Spread of Nationalism*. London: Verso.

Anderson, P. 2005. *Spectrum*. London: Verso.

Appadurai, A. 1990. 'Disjuncture and Difference in the Global Cultural Economy', *Public Culture* 2: 1–24.

Asad, T. 2004. 'Where are the Margins of the State?', in *Anthropology in the Margins of the State*, ed. V. Das and D. Poole. Delhi: Oxford University Press.

Asian Human Rights Commission 2004. 'Second Special Report: Endemic Torture and the Collapse of Policing in Sri Lanka'. *Article 2. Asian Human Rights Commission 3.*

Bailey, F. G. 1963. *Politics and Social Change: Orissa in 1959.* Oxford: Oxford University Press.

 1969. *Stratagems and Spoils: A Social Anthropology of Politics.* Oxford: Blackwell.

Bakhtin, M. 1984. *Rabelais and his World.* Bloomington: Indiana University Press.

Bandaranaike, S. W. R. D. 1963 [1954]. 'The Mystery of the Missing Candidate', in *idem, Speeches and Writings.* Colombo: Dept of Broadcasting and Information.

Barth, F., ed. 1969. *Ethnic Groups and Boundaries: The Social Organization of Culture Difference.* Bergen: Univertsitetsforlaget.

Battaglia, D. 1995. 'Problematizing the Self: A Thematic Introduction', in *Rhetorics of Self-making,* ed. D. Battaglia. Berkeley: University of California Press.

Bauer, J. R., and D. A. Bell, eds. 1999. *The East Asian Challenge for Human Rights.* Cambridge: Cambridge University Press.

Baumann, G. 1995. 'Managing a Polyethnic Milieu: Kinship and Interaction in a London Suburb', *Journal of the Royal Anthropological Institute* 1: 725–41.

 1996. *Contesting Culture: Discourses of Identity in Multi-ethnic London.* Cambridge: Cambridge University Press.

Becker, H. 1967. 'Whose Side Are We On?', *Social Problems* 14: 239–47.

Benjamin, W. 1979 [1920/1]. 'Critique of Violence', in *idem, One-Way Street.* London: New Left Books.

Berlin, I. 1976. *Vico and Herder: Two Studies in the History of Ideas.* London: Hogarth.

Berman, M. 1988. *All that Is Solid Melts into Air: The Experience of Modernity.* New York: Penguin.

Béteille, A. 1965. *Caste, Class and Power: Changing Patterns of Stratification in a Tanjore Village.* Berkeley: University of California Press.

Bloch, M., and J. Parry. 1982. 'Introduction: Death and the Regeneration of Life', in *Death and the Regeneration of Life,* ed. M. Bloch and J. Parry. Cambridge: Cambridge University Press.

Boas, F. 1982 [1898]. *A Franz Boas Reader: The Shaping of American Anthropology, 1883–1911.* Chicago: University of Chicago Press.

Brass, P. R. 1997. *Theft of an Idol: Text and Context in the Representation of Collective Violence.* Princeton, NJ: Princeton University Press.

Bringa, T. 1995. *Being a Muslim the Bosnian Way: Identity and Community in a Central Bosnian Village.* Princeton, NJ: Princeton University Press.

Brow, J. 1978. *Vedda Villages of Anuradhapura: The Historical Anthropology of a Community in Sri Lanka.* Seattle: University of Washington Press.

 1996. *Demons and Development: The Struggle for Community in a Sri Lankan Village.* Tucson: University of Arizona Press.

Bibliography

Burghart, R. 1993. 'His Lordship at the Cobblers' Well', in *An Anthropological Critique of Development: The Growth of Ignorance*, ed. M. Hobart. London: Routledge.

1996. *The Conditions of Listening: Essays on Religion, History, and Politics in South Asia*. Delhi: Oxford University Press.

Carrithers, M., S. Collins, and S. Lukes, eds. 1985. *The Category of the Person: Anthropology, Philosophy, History*. Cambridge: Cambridge University Press.

Chakrabarty, D. 2000. *Provincializing Europe: Postcolonial Thought and Historical Difference*. Princeton, NJ: Princeton University Press.

Chandraprema, C. A. 1991. *Sri Lanka, the Years of Terror: The J.V.P. Insurrection, 1987–1989*. Colombo: Lake House.

Chatterjee, P. 1986. *Nationalist Thought and the Colonial World: A Derivative Discourse?* London: Zed.

1993. *The Nation and its Fragments: Colonial and Postcolonial Histories*. Princeton, NJ: Princeton University Press.

1995. 'Religious Minorities and the Secular State', *Public Culture* 18: 11–39.

Chaudhuri, K. 2001. 'The Ride to Ranchi', in *Frontline*, 25, Dec. 08–21, 2001, available online at http://www.hinduonnet.com/fline/fp1825/18250430.htm, accessed 14 January 2007.

Clifford, J. 1988. *The Predicament of Culture: Twentieth-century Ethnography, Literature and Art*. Cambridge, MA: Harvard University Press.

Cohen, L. 1998. *No Aging in India: Alzheimer's, the Bad Family, and Other Modern Things*. Berkeley: University of California Press.

Coles, K. 2004. 'Election Day: The Construction of Democracy through Technique', *Cultural Anthropology* 19: 551–80.

Comaroff, J. 1985. *Body of Power, Spirit of Resistance: The Culture and History of a South African People*. Chicago: University of Chicago Press.

Corbridge, S., and J. Harriss. 2000. *Reinventing India: Liberalization, Hindu Nationalism and Popular Democracy*. Cambridge: Polity.

Coronil, F. 1995 [1947]. 'Transculturation and the Politics of Theory: Countering the Center Cuban Counterpoint', in F. Ortiz, *Cuban Counterpoint: Tobacco and Sugar*. Durham, NC: Duke University Press.

Crehan, K. 2002. *Gramsci, Culture and Anthropology*. London: Pluto.

Daniel, E. V. 1996. *Charred Lullabies: Chapters in an Anthropography of Violence*. Princeton, NJ: Princeton University Press.

Das, V., ed. 1990a. *Mirrors of Violence: Communities, Riots and Survivors in South Asia*. Delhi: Oxford University Press.

1990b. 'Our Work to Cry, your Work to Listen', in *Mirrors of Violence: Communities, Riots and Survivors in South Asia*, ed. V. Das. Delhi: Oxford University Press.

1995a. 'Communities as Political Actors', in *Critical Events: An Anthropological Perspective on Contemporary India*. Delhi: Oxford University Press.

1995b. *Critical Events: An Anthropological Perspective on Contemporary India*. Delhi: Oxford University Press.

1996. 'The Spatialization of Violence: Case Study of a "Communal Riot"', in *Unravelling the Nation: Sectarian Conflict and India's Secular Identity*, ed. K. Basu and S. Subrahmanyam. Delhi: Penguin.

Das, V., R. K. Das, M. Manoranjan, and A. Nandy. 1984. 'A New Kind of Rioting', *Illustrated Weekly of India*, 23 December 1984: 20–3.

Das, V., and D. Poole. 2004. 'State and its Margins: Comparative Ethnographies', in *Anthropology in the Margins of the State*, ed. V. Das and D. Poole. Delhi: Oxford University Press.

Davies, C. 2000. 'Fernando Ortiz's Transculturation: The Postcolonial Intellectual and the Politics of Cultural Representation', in *Postcolonial Perspectives on the Cultures of Latin America and Lusophone Africa*, ed. R. Fiddian. Liverpool: Liverpool University Press.

Davies, C., and R. Fardon. 1991. 'African Fictions in Representations of West African and Afro-Cuban Culture', *Bulletin of the John Rylands Library Manchester* 73: 125–45.

de Silva, K. M. 1973. 'The History and Politics of the Transfer of Power', in *University of Ceylon History of Ceylon. 3: From the Beginning of the 19th Century to 1948*, ed. K. M. de Silva. Peradeniya: University of Ceylon Press Board.

Dickey, S. 1993. 'The Politics of Adulation: Cinema and the Production of Politicians in South India', *Journal of Asian Studies* 52: 340–72.

Dumont, L. 1980. *Homo Hierarchicus: The Caste System and its Implications*. Chicago: University of Chicago Press.

Dunn, J. 1980. 'From Democracy to Representation: An Interpretation of a Ghanaian Election', in *idem, Political Obligation in its Historical Context: Essays in Political Theory*. Cambridge: Cambridge University Press.

1992. 'Preface', in *Democracy: The Unfinished Journey, 508 BC to AD 1993*, ed. J. Dunn. Oxford: Oxford University Press.

Easton, D. 1959. 'Political Anthropology', *Biennial Review of Anthropology* 1: 210–62.

Edelman, M. 1985. *The Symbolic Uses of Politics*. Urbana: University of Illinois Press.

Fabian, J. 1983. *Time and the Other: How Anthropology Makes its Object*. New York: Columbia University Press.

Ferguson, J. 1999. *Expectations of Modernity: Myths and Meanings of Urban Life on the Zambian Copperbelt*. Berkeley: University of California Press.

Bibliography

Fortes, M., and E. E. Evans-Pritchard. 1940. 'Introduction', in *African Political Systems*, ed. M. Fortes and E. E. Evans-Pritchard. London: Oxford University Press for the International African Institute.

Foucault, M. 1967 [1961]. *Madness and Civilization: A History of Insanity in the Age of Reason*. London: Tavistock.

——— 1974 [1966]. *The Order of Things: An Archaeology of the Human Sciences*. London: Routledge.

——— 1977. *Discipline and Punish: The Birth of the Prison*. London: Allen Lane.

——— 1991a. 'On Governmentality', in *The Foucault Effect: Studies in Governmentality*, ed. G. Burchell, C. Gordon, and P. Miller. London: Harvester Wheatsheaf.

——— 1991b. 'Questions of Method', in *The Foucault Effect: Studies in Governmentality*, ed. G. Burchell, C. Gordon, and P. Miller. Chicago: University of Chicago Press.

Fox, R. G. 1969. *From Zamindar to Ballot-Box: Community Change in a North Indian Market Town*. Ithaca: Cornell University Press.

Geertz, C. 1973. *The Interpretation of Cultures: Selected Essays*. New York: Basic Books.

——— 2000. *Available Light: Anthropological Reflections on Philosophical Topics*. Princeton, NJ: Princeton University Press.

Gellner, D. N., ed. 2003. *Resistance and the State: Nepalese Experiences*. Delhi: Social Science Press.

Ghosh, A. 1992. *In an Antique Land*. London: Granta.

——— 1993. 'The Slave of MS. H. 6', in *Subaltern Studies VII: Writings on South Asian History and Society*, ed. P. Chatterjee and G. Pandey. Delhi: Oxford University Press.

Gilroy, P. 1993. *The Black Atlantic: Modernity and Double Consciousness*. London: Verso.

Gluckman, M. 1949. 'Malinowski's Sociological Theories', *Rhodes-Livingstone Paper* 16.

Gombrich, R. 1971. *Precept and Practice: Traditional Buddhism in the Rural Highlands of Ceylon*. Oxford: Clarendon Press.

Gombrich, R., and G. Obeyesekere. 1988. *Buddhism Transformed: Religious Change in Sri Lanka*. Princeton, NJ: Princeton University Press.

Goonatilake, S. 2001. *Anthropologizing Sri Lanka: A Eurocentric Misadventure*. Bloomington: Indiana University Press.

Gould, H. A. 2003. 'Local-level/Grassroots Political Studies', in *Oxford India Companion to Sociology and Social Anthropology*, vol. II, ed. V. Das. Delhi: Oxford University Press.

Guha, R. 1982a. 'On Some Aspects of the Historiography of Colonial India', in *Subaltern Studies I: Writings on South Asian History and Society*, ed. R. Guha. Delhi: Oxford University Press.

1982b. 'Preface', in *Subaltern Studies I: Writings on South Asian History and Society*, ed. R. Guha. Delhi: Oxford University Press.

1983. *Elementary Aspects of Peasant Insurgency in Colonial India*. Delhi: Oxford University Press.

1989. 'Dominance without Hegemony and its Historiography', in *Subaltern Studies VI: Writings on South Asian History and Society*, ed. R. Guha. Delhi: Oxford University Press.

1997. 'Introduction', in *A Subaltern Studies Reader, 1986–1995*, ed. R. Guha. Minneapolis: University of Minnesota Press.

Gupta, A. 1995. 'Blurred Boundaries: The Discourse of Corruption, the Culture of Politics, and the Imagined State', *American Ethnologist* 22: 375–402.

Hacking, I. 1999. *The Social Construction of What?* Cambridge, MA: Harvard University Press.

Hall, S. and T. Jefferson, eds. 1976. *Resistance through Rituals: Youth Subcultures in Post-war Britain*. London: Hutchinson.

Handler, R. 1988. *Nationalism and the Politics of Culture in Quebec*. Madison, WI: University of Wisconsin Press.

Hannerz, U. 1987. 'The World in Creolisation', *Africa* 57(4): 546–59.

1992. *Cultural Complexity: Studies in the Social Organization of Meaning*. New York: Columbia University Press.

Hansen, T. B. 1997. 'Inside the Romanticist Episteme', *Thesis Eleven* 48: 21–42.

1999. *The Saffron Wave: Democracy and Hindu Nationalism in Modern India*. Princeton, NJ: Princeton University Press.

2000. 'Predicaments of Secularism: Muslim Identities and Politics in Mumbai', *Journal of the Royal Anthropological Institute* 6: 255–72.

2001a. 'Governance and Myths of State in Mumbai', in *The Everyday State and Society in Modern India*, ed. C. J. Fuller and V. Bénéï. London: Hurst.

2001b. *Wages of Violence: Naming and Identity in Postcolonial Bombay*. Princeton, NJ: Princeton University Press.

2005. 'Sovereigns beyond the State: On Legality and Authority in Urban India', in *Sovereign Bodies: Citizens, Migrants, and States in the Postcolonial World*, ed. T. B. Hansen and F. Stepputat. Princeton, NJ: Princeton University Press.

Hardiman, D. 1982. 'The Indian "Faction": A Political Theory Examined', in *Subaltern Studies I: Writings on South Asian History and Society*, ed. R. Guha. Delhi: Oxford University Press.

Hefner, R. W. 2000. *Civil Islam: Muslims and Democratization in Indonesia*. Princeton, NJ: Princeton University Press.

Herzfeld, M. 1986. *Ours Once More: Folklore, Ideology, and the Making of Modern Greece*. New York: Pella.

Bibliography

Hirschman, A. O. 1977. *The Passions and the Interests: Political Arguments for Capitalism before its Triumph.* Princeton, NJ: Princeton University Press.

Hocart, A. M. 1970. *Kings and Councillors: An Essay in the Comparative Anatomy of Human Society.* Chicago: University of Chicago Press.

Hoole, R. 2001. *Sri Lanka: The Arrogance of Power. Myths, Decadence and Murder.* Colombo: University Teachers for Human Rights (Jaffna).

Horowitz, D. L. 2001. *The Deadly Ethnic Riot.* Berkeley: University of California Press.

Humphrey, C. 2004. 'Sovereignty', in *A Companion to the Anthropology of Politics*, ed. D. Nugent and J. Vincent. Oxford: Blackwell.

Huntington, S. 1993. 'The Clash of Civilizations?', *Foreign Affairs* 72: 22–49.

James, W. 1973. 'The Anthropologist as Reluctant Imperialist', in *Anthropology and the Colonial Encounter*, ed. T. Asad. London: Ithaca.

Jayawardena, K. 1985. *Ethnicity and Class Conflicts in Sri Lanka.* Colombo: Sanjiva.

Jeffery, P. 2001. 'A "Uniform Customary Code"? Marital Breakdown and Women's Economic Entitlements in Rural Bijnor', *Contributions to Indian Sociology*, 35(1): 1–32.

Jeganathan, P. 1996. 'All the Lord's Men?', in *Sri Lanka: Collective Identities Revisited*, vol. II, ed. M. Roberts. Colombo: Marga.

Kakar, S. 1996. *The Colors of Violence: Cultural Identities, Religion, and Conflict.* Chicago: University of Chicago Press.

Kantorowicz, E. H. 1958. *The King's Two Bodies: A Study in Medieval Political Theology.* Princeton, NJ: Princeton University Press.

Kapferer, B. 1983. *A Celebration of Demons: Exorcism and the Aesthetics of Healing in Sri Lanka.* Bloomington: Indiana University Press.

1988. *Legends of People, Myths of State: Violence, Intolerance and Political Culture in Sri Lanka and Australia.* Washington, DC: Smithsonian Institution Press.

Kaviraj, S. 1992. 'The Imaginary Institution of India', in *Subaltern Studies VII*, ed. P. Chatterjee and G. Pandey. Delhi: Oxford University Press.

1998. 'The Culture of Representative Democracy', in *Wages of Freedom: Fifty Years of the Indian Nation-State*, ed. P. Chatterjee. Delhi: Oxford University Press.

Kemp, C. 1984. 'Politics and Class, in Spring Valley, Sri Lanka – An Anti-structuralist Interpretation', *Journal of Peasant Studies* 12: 41–64.

Kemper, S. 1991. *The Presence of the Past: Chronicles, Politics and Culture in Sinhala Life.* Ithaca: Cornell University Press.

Khilnani, S. 1997. *The Idea of India.* London: Hamish Hamilton.

Kymlicka, W. 1995. *Multicultural Citizenship: A Liberal Theory of Minority Rights.* Oxford: Clarendon Press.

Laidlaw, J. 2002. 'For an Anthropology of Ethics and Freedom', *Journal of the Royal Anthropological Institute* 8: 311–32.

Latour, B. 1993. *We Have Never Been Modern.* London: Harvester-Wheatsheaf.

Lave, J. D., P. Duguid, N. Fernandez, and E. Axel. 1992. 'Coming of Age in Birmingham: Cultural Studies and Conceptions of Subjectivity', *Annual Review of Anthropology* 21: 257–82.

Leach, E. R. 1954. *Political Systems of Highland Burma: A Study of Kachin Social Structure*. London: Athlone.

1961. *Pul Eliya, a Village in Ceylon: A Study of Land Tenure and Kinship*. Cambridge: Cambridge University Press.

2002 [1961]. 'The Troubles of Ranhamy Ge Punchirala (X:4)', in *The Anthropology of Politics: A Reader in Ethnography, Theory and Critique*, ed. J. Vincent. Oxford: Blackwell.

Lefort, C. 1986. *The Political Forms of Modern Society: Bureaucracy, Democracy, Totalitarianism*. Cambridge: Polity.

1988. *Democracy and Political Theory*. Cambridge: Polity.

Lilla, M. 2001. *The Restless Mind: Intellectuals in Politics*. New York: New York Review Books.

Ludden, D. 2001. 'Subalterns and Others in the Agrarian History of South Asia', in *Agrarian Studies: Synthetic Work at the Cutting Edge*, ed. J. C. B. Scott and Nina Bhatt. New Haven: Yale.

Lukes, S. 1975. 'Political Ritual and Social Integration', *Sociology* 9: 289–308.

McGilvray, D. 1982. 'Mukkuvar Vannimai: Tamil Caste and Matriclan Structure in Batticaloa, Sri Lanka', in *Caste Ideology and Interaction, Cambridge Papers in Social Anthropology* 9, ed. D. McGilvray. Cambridge: Cambridge University Press.

1998. 'Arabs, Moors and Muslims: Sri Lankan Muslim Ethnicity in Regional Perspective', *Contributions to Indian Sociology* 32: 433–83.

Machiavelli, N. 1988. *The Prince. Cambridge Texts in the History of Political Thought*. Cambridge: Cambridge University Press.

MacIntyre, A. 1971. 'Is a Science of Comparative Politics Possible?', in *idem, Against the Self-images of the Age: Essays on Ideology and Philosophy*. London: Duckworth.

Mahmood, C. K. 1996. *Fighting for Faith and Nation: Dialogues with Sikh Militants*. Philadelphia: University of Pennsylvania Press.

Mahmood, S. 2001. 'Feminist Theory, Embodiment, and the Docile Agent: Some Reflections on the Egyptian Islamic Revival', *Cultural Anthropology* 16: 202–36.

Malinowski, B. 1935. *Coral Gardens and their Magic: A Study of the Methods of Tilling the Soil and of Agricultural Rites in the Trobriand Islands / Vol. 1, The Description of Gardening*, vol. I. London: Allen & Unwin.

1938. 'Introduction', in *Methods of Study of Culture Contact in Africa*, ed. B. Malinowski. London: Oxford University Press for the International Institute of African Languages and Cultures.

Bibliography

1945. *The Dynamics of Culture Change: An Inquiry into Race Relations in Africa.* New Haven: Yale University Press.

1995 [1947]. 'Introduction', in F. Ortiz, *Cuban Counterpoint: Tobacco and Sugar.* Durham, NC: Duke University Press.

Mann, M. 2005. *The Dark Side of Democracy: Explaining Ethnic Cleansing.* Cambridge: Cambridge University Press.

Manor, J., ed. 1984. *Sri Lanka: In Change and Crisis.* London: Croom Helm.

Mbembe, A. 1992. 'Provisional notes on the postcolony', *Africa* 62: 3–37.

Mendis, G. C., ed. 1956. *The Colebrooke-Cameron Papers: Documents on British Colonial Policy in Ceylon 1796–1833.* Oxford: Oxford University Press.

Merton, R. 1957 [1937]. 'The Self-fulfilling Prophecy', in *idem, Social Theory and Social Structure: Toward the Codification of Theory and Research.* Glencoe, IL: Free Press.

Meyer, E. 1984. 'Seeking the Roots of the Tragedy', in *Sri Lanka: In Change and Crisis,* ed. J. Manor. London: Croom Helm.

Michelutti, L. 2004. '"We (Yadavs) Are a Caste of Politicians": Caste and Modern Politics in a North Indian Town', *Contributions to Indian Sociology* 38: 43–72.

Millard, C. 2003. 'Perceptions of Democracy and Dissent in the Valley of Dhorpatan', in *Resistance and the State: Nepalese Experiences,* ed. D. N. Gellner. Delhi: Social Science Press.

Mitchell, T. 1991. 'The Limits of the State: Beyond Statist Approaches and their Critics', *American Political Science Review* 85: 77–96.

Moore, M. 1993. 'Thoroughly Modern Revolutionaries: The JVP in Sri Lanka', *Modern Asian Studies* 27 (3): 593–642.

Mouffe, C. 2000. *The Democratic Paradox.* London: Verso.

Nairn, T. 1981. *The Break-up of Britain.* London: Verso.

Nanayakkara, S. 2004. *Jathika Chinthanaya.* Boralesgamuwa: Young Socialist Publication.

Navaro-Yashin, Y. 2002. *Faces of the State: Secularism and Public Life in Turkey.* Princeton, NJ: Princeton University Press.

Nicholas, R. 1968. 'Structures of Politics in the Villages of Southern Asia', in *Structure and Change in Indian Society,* ed. M. Singer and B. Cohn. Chicago: Aldine.

Nordstrom, C. 1995. 'War on the Front Lines', in *Fieldwork under Fire: Contemporary Studies of Violence and Survival,* ed. C. Nordstrom and A. C. G. M. Robben. Berkeley: University of California Press.

Nugent, D., and J. Vincent, eds. 2004. *A Companion to the Anthropology of Politics.* Oxford: Blackwell.

Obeyesekere, G. 1967. *Land Tenure in Village Ceylon: A Sociological and Historical Study.* Cambridge: Cambridge University Press.

1981. *Medusa's Hair: An Essay on Personal Symbols and Religious Experience.* Chicago: University of Chicago Press.

1984. 'The Origins and Institutionalisation of Political Violence', in *Sri Lanka: In Change and Crisis*, ed. J. Manor. London: Croom Helm.

Ong, A. 1987. *Spirits of Resistance and Capitalist Discipline: Factory Women in Malaysia.* Albany: State University of New York Press.

Ortiz, F. 1995 [1947]. *Cuban Counterpoint: Tobacco and Sugar.* Durham, NC: Duke University Press.

Ortner, S. 1995. 'Resistance and the Problem of Ethnographic Refusal', *Comparative Studies in Society and History* 37: 173–93.

Paley, J. 2002. 'Toward an Anthropology of Democracy', *Annual Review of Anthropology* 31: 469–96.

2004. 'Accountable Democracy: Citizens' Impact on Public Decision Making in Postdictatorship Chile', *American Ethnologist* 31: 497–513.

Pandey, G. 1990. *The Construction of Communalism in Colonial North India.* Delhi: Oxford University Press.

Pandian, M. S. S. 1992. *The Image Trap: MG Ramachandram in Film and Politics.* New Delhi: Sage.

Pels, P., J.-L. Briquet and R. Bertrand, eds. 2007. *Cultures of Voting: The Hidden History of the Secret Ballot.* London: Hurst.

Pérez Firmat, G. 1989. *The Cuban Condition: Translation and Identity in Modern Cuban Literature.* Cambridge: Cambridge University Press.

Presidential Commission on Youth. 1990. *Report of the Presidential Commission on Youth.* Government of Sri Lanka.

Radcliffe-Brown, A. R. 1940. 'Preface', in *African Political Systems*, ed. M. Fortes and E. E. Evans-Pritchard. London: Oxford University Press for the International African Institute.

Rawls, J. 1993. *Political Liberalism.* New York: Columbia University Press.

Richards, P. 1996. *Fighting for the Rainforest: War, Youth and Resources in Sierra Leone.* Oxford: James Currey.

Robinson, M. S. 1975. *Political Structure in a Changing Sinhalese Village.* Cambridge: Cambridge University Press.

Rorty, R. 1998. *Achieving our Country: Leftist Thought in Twentieth-century America.* Cambridge, MA: Harvard University Press.

Russell, J. 1982. *Communal Politics under the Donoughmore Constitution, 1931–47.* Dehiwela: Tissa Prakasakayo.

Ruud, A. E. 2001. 'Talking Dirty about Politics: A View from a Bengali Village', in *The Everyday State and Society in Modern India*, ed. C. J. Fuller and V. Bénéï. London: Hurst.

Bibliography

Sahlins, M. 1976. *Culture and Practical Reason.* Chicago: University of Chicago Press.

1985. *Islands of History.* Chicago: University of Chicago Press.

1999. 'Two or Three Things I Know about Culture', *Journal of the Royal Anthropological Institute* 5: 399–421.

2002. *Waiting for Foucault, Still.* Chicago: Prickly Paradigm Press.

1978. *Orientalism.* London: Routledge and Kegan Paul.

Samaddar, R. 1999. *The Marginal Nation: Transborder Migration from Bangladesh to West Bengal.* New Delhi: Sage.

Sarachchandra, E. R. 1978. *Curfew and a Full Moon.* Singapore: Heinemann.

Schmitt, C. 1996 [1932]. *The Concept of the Political.* Chicago: University of Chicago Press.

Scott, D. 1990. 'The Demonology of Nationalism: On the Anthropology of Ethnicity and Violence in Sri Lanka', *Economy and Society* 19: 491–510.

1995. 'Colonial Governmentality', *Social Text* 43: 191–220.

1999. *Refashioning Futures: Criticism after Postcoloniality.* Princeton, NJ: Princeton University Press.

Scott, J. C. 1976. *The Moral Economy of the Peasant: Rebellion and Subsistence in Southeast Asia.* New Haven: Yale University Press.

1985. *Weapons of the Weak: Everyday Forms of Peasant Resistance.* New Haven: Yale University Press.

1998. *Seeing like a State: How Certain Schemes to Improve the Human Condition have Failed.* New Haven: Yale University Press.

Sen, A. 1997. 'Human Rights and Asian Values', *Sixteenth Morgenthau Memorial Lecture on Ethics & Foreign Policy, 1997.* Available online at http://www.cceia.org/resources/publications/morgenthau/254.html, accessed 13 January 2007.

Seneviratne, H. L. 1976. *Rituals of the Kandyan State.* Cambridge: Cambridge University Press.

1999. *The Work of Kings: The New Buddhism in Sri Lanka.* Chicago: University of Chicago Press.

Spencer, J. 1984. 'Popular Perceptions of the Violence: A Provincial View', in *Sri Lanka: In Change and Crisis*, ed. J. Manor. London: Croom Helm.

1989. Review of Kapferer *Legends of People, Myths of State*, *Man* 24: 179–80.

1990a. 'Collective Violence and Everyday Practice in Sri Lanka', *Modern Asian Studies* 24 (3): 603–23.

1990b. *A Sinhala Village in a Time of Trouble: Politics and Change in Rural Sri Lanka.* Delhi: Oxford University Press.

1990c. 'Writing Within: Anthropology, Nationalism, and Culture in Sri Lanka', *Current Anthropology* 31: 283–330.

1997a. 'Fatima and the Enchanted Toffees: An Essay on Contingency, Narrative and Therapy', *Journal of the Royal Anthropological Institute* 3: 693–710.

1997b. 'Post-colonialism and the Political Imagination', *Journal of the Royal Anthropological Institute* 3: 1–19.

2000. 'On not Becoming a Terrorist: Problems of Memory, Agency and Community in the Sri Lankan Conflict', in *Violence and Subjectivity*, ed. V. Das, A. Kleinman, M. Ramphele, and P. Reynolds. Berkeley: University of California Press.

2003. 'A Nation "Living in Different Places": Notes on the Impossible Work of Purification in Postcolonial Sri Lanka', *Contributions to Indian Sociology* 37 (1/2): 1–23.

Spivak, G. C. 2002 [1992]. 'Thinking Academic Freedom in Gendered Post-coloniality', in *The Anthropology of Politics: A Reader in Ethnography, Theory and Critique*, ed. J. Vincent. Oxford: Blackwell.

Stirrat, R. L. 1984. 'The Riots and Roman Catholic Church in Historical Perspective', in *Sri Lanka: In Change and Crisis*, ed. J. Manor. London: Croom Helm.

1988. *On the Beach: Fishermen, Fishwives and Fishtraders in Post-colonial Sri Lanka*. Delhi: Hindustan.

1992. *Power and Religiosity in a Post-colonial Setting: Sinhala Catholics in Contemporary Sri Lanka*. Cambridge: Cambridge University Press.

Stocking, G. 1983. 'The Ethnographer's Magic: Fieldwork in British Anthropology from Tylor to Malinowski', in *Observers Observed: Essays on Ethnographic Fieldwork, History of Anthropology* I, ed. G. Stocking. Madison, WI: University of Wisconsin Press.

1991. 'Maclay, Kubary, Malinowski: Archetypes from the Dreamtime of Anthropology', in *Colonial Situations: Essays on the Contextualization of Ethnographic Knowledge, History of Anthropology* VII, ed. G. Stocking. Madison, WI: University of Wisconsin Press.

Strathern, M. 1987. 'An Awkward Relationship: The Case of Feminism and Anthropology', *Signs* 12: 276–92.

1988. *The Gender of the Gift: Problems with Women and Problems with Society in Melanesia*. Berkeley: University of California Press.

Tambiah, S. J. 1976. *World Conqueror and World Renouncer : A Study of Buddhism and Polity in Thailand against a Historical Background*. Cambridge: Cambridge University Press.

1992. *Buddhism Betrayed?: Religion, Politics, and Violence in Sri Lanka*. Chicago: University of Chicago Press.

1996. *Leveling Crowds: Ethnonationalist Conflicts and Collective Violence in South Asia*. Berkeley: University of California Press.

Bibliography

Tarlo, E. 2000. 'Body and Space in a Time of Crisis: Sterilization and Resettlement during the Emergency in Delhi', in *Violence and Subjectivity*, ed. V. Das, A. Kleinman, M. Ramphele, and P. Reynolds. Berkeley: University of California Press.

— 2001. 'Paper Truths: The Emergency and Slum Clearance through Forgotten Files', in *The Everyday State and Society in Modern India*, ed. C. J. Fuller and V. Bénéï. London: Hurst.

— 2003. *Unsettling Memories: Narratives of the Emergency in Delhi*. London: Hurst.

Taussig, M. T. 1992. 'Maleficium: State Fetishism', in *idem, The Nervous System*. New York: Routledge.

— 1997. *The Magic of the State*. New York: Routledge.

Taylor, C. 1985a [1971]. 'Interpretation and the Sciences of Man', in *idem, Philosophy and the Human Sciences: Philosophical Papers 2*. Cambridge: Cambridge University Press.

— 1985b. *Philosophy and the Human Sciences: Philosophical Papers 2*. Cambridge: Cambridge University Press.

— 1992. *Multiculturalism and 'The Politics of Recognition': An Essay*. Princeton, NJ: Princeton University Press.

— 1995. 'Preface', in *idem, Philosophical Arguments*. Cambridge, MA: Harvard University Press.

Thompson, E. P. 1963. *The Making of the English Working Class*. London: Gollancz.

Trawick, M. 1999. 'Reasons for Violence: A Preliminary Ethnographic Account of the LTTE', in *Conflict and Community in Contemporary Sri Lanka. 'Pearl of the East' or the 'Island of Tears'?*, ed. S. Gamage and I. B. Watson. Colombo: Vijitha Yapa.

Turner, V. 1957. *Schism and Continuity in an African Society: A Study of Ndembu Life*. Manchester: Manchester University Press.

Uyangoda, J. 1997. 'Academic Texts on the Sri Lankan Ethnic Question as Biographies of a Decaying Nation-state', *Nethra* 1: 7–23.

van der Veer, P. 1992. 'Playing or Praying: A Sufi Saint's Day in Surat', *Journal of Asian Studies* 51: 545–64.

Vincent, J. 1990. *Anthropology and Politics: Visions, Traditions, and Trends*. Tucsan: University of Arizona Press.

— 1996a. 'Plural society', in *Encyclopedia of Social and Cultural Anthropology*, ed. A. Barnard and J. Spencer. London: Routledge.

— 1996b. 'Political Anthropology', in *Encyclopedia of Social and Cultural Anthropology*, ed. A. Barnard and J. Spencer, pp. 428–34. London: Routledge.

— ed. 2002. *The Anthropology of Politics: A Reader in Ethnography, Theory and Critique*. Oxford: Blackwell.

Weber, M. 1978. *Economy and Society*, vol. 1. Berkeley: University of California Press.

Bibliography

West, H. 2005. '"Govern Yourselves!" Democracy and Carnage in Northern Mozambique.' Unpublished conference paper, presented at the School of American Research Advanced Seminar 'Towards an Anthropology of Democracy', Santa Fe, 6–10 March.

Wickramasinghe, M. 1973 [1952]. *Aspects of Sinhalese Culture*, 3rd edn. Dehiwala: Tissa Prakasakayo.

1975 [1971]. 'Culture and Tradition', in *idem, Sinhala Language and Culture*. Dehiwala: Tissa Prakasakayo.

Williams, R. 1958. *Culture and Society 1780–1950*. London: Chatto & Windus.

1977. *Marxism and Literature*. Oxford: Oxford University Press.

Willis, P. 1977. *Learning to Labour: How Working-class Kids Get Working-class Jobs*. Aldershot: Gower.

Wilson, R. 2001. *The Politics of Truth and Reconciliation in South Africa: Legitimizing the Post-apartheid State*. Cambridge: Cambridge University Press.

Wimmer, A. 2002. *Nationalist Exclusion and Ethnic Conflict: Shadows of Modernity*. Cambridge: Cambridge University Press.

Wimmer, A., and N. Glick Schiller. 2002. 'Methodological Nationalism and Beyond: Nation-state Building, Migration and the Social Sciences', *Global Networks* 4: 301–34.

Woost, M. 1994. Review of Kapferer *Legends of People Myths of State, American Ethnologist* 21: 912–14.

Yalman, N. 1967. *Under the Bo Tree: Studies in Caste, Kinship, and Marriage in the Interior of Ceylon*. Berkeley: University of California Press.

Index

Index